FREE LIKE SPINOZA

An Introduction to Ethics

Denis Collin

FREE LIKE SPINOZA

An Introduction to Ethics

Max Milo Éditions, Paris, 2023

www.maxmilo.com

ISBN : 978-2-315-01265-7

WARNING

There are many editions of Spinoza's works, but no complete scientific edition. The Presses universitaires de France have undertaken this work under the direction of Pierre-François Moreau (*Premiers écrits. Œuvres complètes I*, 2009; *Traité théologico-politique*, 2012), but the major work, *Ethics,* is still missing. However, we do have a good edition, published by Gallimard in the "Bibliothèque de la Pléiade" collection (*Œuvres complètes*, Pléiade no. 108, 1954). It is the translation of this edition that we will use here. But as no translation is perfect, we also recommend Bernard Pautrat's precise but sometimes rough translation, published by Editions du Seuil *(Éthique,* bilingual Latin-French edition, 2010). Robert Misrahi's translation, published by Éditions de l'Éclat (2005), is also very good. Charles Appuhn's (Garnier-Flammarion, 1965) is a fine reference. But since translation is a betrayal, it should be possible to read the *Ethics* in Latin, as recommended by the commentator Pierre Macherey. For Spinoza's other works, I have left out the titles of the Pléiade edition and kept the classic titles: *Traité de la réforme de l'entendement* (and not *Traité de l'amendement de l'intellect*), *Traité politique* (and not *Traité des autorités politiques*), *Traité théologico-politique* and not *Traité des autorités théologiques et politiques*.

To simplify references to the *Ethics,* the commonly used abbreviations are given below. For references to other books by Spinoza: TRE5 refers to paragraph 5 of the *Traité de la réforme de l'entendement*, TP to the *Traité politique*, and TTP to the *Traité théologico-politique*.

There are a great many references to the text, which may seem to make it more cumbersome to read. But how can we do otherwise if our object is to read a text that itself systematically uses references: Spinoza's *Ethics* is the first work in hypertext!

Convention for *Ethics* abbreviations

- We use E when a reference is abbreviated to one of the five **parts** of the *Ethics, for* example, E1 for *Ethics* I or E5 for *Ethics* V.

- For **definitions,** D1 for definition I, D2 for definition II, D3 for definition III, etc.

- For **axioms,** A1 for axiom I, A2 for axiom II, A3 for axiom III, etc.

- For **appendices,** E1A for the appendix to Part 1, E4A chap. XXXII, for example, for the appendix to Part 4, chapter XXXII.

- For **propositions,** this would be E1P16 for *Ethics* I, proposition XVI, or E4P27 for *Ethics* IV, proposition XXVII, etc.

- **Demonstrations** are not abbreviated.

- For **corollaries,** this would be E3P1C for *Ethics* III, proposition I, corollary, and when there are several corollaries, this would be E1P16C1 for *Ethics* I, proposition XVI, corollary I, or E1P16C3 for *Ethics* I, proposition XVI, corollary III, and so on.

- For **scolies,** this will be E2P10S for *Ethics* II, proposition X, scolie, and when there are several scolies, this will be E4P37S1 for *Ethics* IV, proposition XXXVII, scolie I, or E4P37S2 for *Ethics* IV, proposition XXXVII, scolie II.

Introduction

When he died on February 21, 1677, in his forty-fifth year, suffering from phthisis, from which he had been suffering for a long time, Spinoza left his masterwork, the *Ethics, in* manuscript form. It was first published after his death by Lodewijk Meyer (or Meijer), a doctor and trusted friend of Spinoza. Although Spinoza was not a prolific writer (his works can be found in a single volume of the Pléiade), his *Ethics is* a major work, one of the greatest books in the history of philosophy, and an ever-vital source from which philosophers continue to draw. Hegel, in his *History of Philosophy,* underlines its importance: "Spinoza is the capital point of modern philosophy: either Spinozism, or no philosophy" (*Vorlesungen über die Geschichte der Philosophie,* in *Werke,* E. Moldenhauer and K.M. Michel (eds.), Frankfurt am Main, Suhrkamp, 1986, vol. 20, p. 164). But Hegel's enthusiasm, which can be found in the introduction to the second edition of the *Encyclopédie des sciences philosophiques,* does not prevent a systematic critique of the limits of Spinozism. Bergson is often quoted as writing to Léon Brunschvicg in 1927: "Every philosopher has two philosophies: his own and Spinoza's." But in 1928, in a letter to Jankélévitch, the tone is a little different: "I think I've told you that I always feel a little at home when I reread the *Ethics,* and that I'm surprised every time, since most of my theses seem to be (and indeed are, in my thinking) the opposite of Spinozism." If Spinoza appears to be the nexus of all modern philosophy, threads run in all directions from this nexus. With Diderot or d'Holbach, we have a materialist Spinozism, while Hegel pulls it in a completely different direction. Alain's Spinoza has no real connection with Toni Negri's. Does Martial Guéroult's Spinoza meet Pierre Macherey's? This, it may be said, is the fate of all great philosophies. There was a right-wing Hegelianism and a left-wing Hegelianism. Kant was turned into a conservative moralist as well as a republican sympathetic to the cause of the French Revolution. So we have a revolutionary Spinoza backing up declining Marxists, and a paradoxically conservative Spinoza. One protest economist takes Spinoza as his guide in a new critique of the capitalist mode of production (see Frédéric Lordon, *Capitalisme, désir et servitude. Marx et Spinoza,* La fabrique, 2010). For others, Spinoza is a good medication against stress (Héloïse Guay de Bellissen, *Spinoza antistress en 99 pilules philosophiques,* Les Éditions de l'Opportun, 2012). That's a lot for one man.

It could be said that this man, who for part of his life lived very modestly by his trade—he polished lentils—and published very little during his lifetime, has enjoyed a posthumous fame that has not waned: here is a figure of genius ignored by his contemporaries and to whom posterity gives its due. But Spinoza was already famous in his own lifetime. A paradoxical celebrity for a man who never sought fame and praised prudence as a practical virtue: *Caute* was his motto. Sulphurous celebrity. Published anonymously under a false publisher's name, the *Traité théologico-politique* earned him a solidly bad reputation. This treatise, it's true, considers the Bible as a human work and not a "sacred" text, attempts to understand its properly political reason, and ends with a defense of the freedom to think without having to submit to religious authority. Very quickly known throughout Europe, this text earned its author a reputation as an atheist, and even created a literary genre: the refutation of the "Spinoza atheist". But Spinoza also had a reputation as one of the greatest minds of his time. Leibniz sought him out and met him in November 1676, in The Hague. Leibniz was 30 years old, and it was a decisive visit. Leibniz was fascinated by Spinoza's system, and his entire work can be read as an attempt to provide answers to the fundamental questions posed by Spinoza: if the deterministic conception of reality is true, how can man still be said to possess free will? What room is left for morality, piety and so on? What relationship does the soul (or spirit) have with the body? Leibniz and Spinoza were both confronted with Descartes' work and the irruption of modern Galilean physics. They both sought to draw all the consequences, and the confrontation of these two major works continues to enlighten us.

But Leibniz would never boast of this visit, nor of his interest in this well-known "atheist". Leibniz wanted to be a diplomat, a man of the court who associated with the powerful, and Spinoza was a heretic indifferent to honors and money. He could have had either. Jean Colerus relates this anecdote, among many others: "Simon De Vries, of Amsterdam, who shows great attachment to him in the twenty-sixth letter and at the same time calls him his very faithful friend (*amice integerrime*), one day presented him with a sum of two thousand florins, to put him in a position to live a little more comfortably ; but Spinoza, in the presence of his host, civilly apologized for not being able to receive this money, on the pretext that he needed nothing, and that so much money, if he received it, would infallibly divert him from his studies and occupations" (Johannes Colerus, *Vie de Spinoza* (1706), *in* Colerus/Lucas, *Vies de Spinoza*, Éditions Allia, 1999, p. 43). In 1673, an emissary of the Prince of Condé had informed Spinoza that the Prince wished to offer him a pension provided he agreed to dedicate some work to the King of France, a proposal Spinoza declined with all his customary courtesy. In the same year, the Elector Palatine wanted to lure him to Heidelberg to teach philosophy: again, he declined.

Spinoza lived by the precepts he sets out at the beginning of his *Treatise on the Reform of the Understanding*: renounce glory, money and honors in search of a stable sovereign good, which can ultimately only be found in the knowledge of God, things and oneself. However, the image of an ascetic philosopher withdrawn from the world doesn't fit either. He was a highly sociable man, involved in the political and theological discussions of his day, and never concealed his republican convictions. In his works, he always sought to show the practical and political consequences of his philosophy. His unfinished *Treatise on Politics* praises politicians as practical men who base themselves solely on experience, in contrast to philosophers, theo-logists and other moralists who praise a man who exists nowhere, and fabricate utopias to better mortify the man who actually exists. A little book in which the reference, both explicit and implicit, to Machiavelli is constant. So constant, in fact, that it's easy to say: Machiavelli, Spinoza, same battle! For those unfamiliar with Machiavelli's thought, and who confine themselves to the calumnies of a Frederick II, the connection seems incongruous, yet it is indeed the "most penetrating Florentine" who inspires Spinoza's politics.

Of course, it's impossible to cover all of Spinoza's thought here. There is much that is good and deeply illuminating in this powerful work, including the correspondence, which often provides indispensable insights. But it is the *Ethics* that must be read, meditated upon and copied. Written between 1661 and 1675, and published only after his death, this work is a world of its own, never to be completed. And that's where we need to enter. The path is a difficult one, as the scolie of the last proposition of the fifth part of the *Ethics* acknowledges: "If, it is true, the path I have just indicated seems very arduous, one can nevertheless find it" (E5P42S).

CHAPTER I:
"ON GOD" OR THE NATURE OF THINGS DEMONSTRATED *ORDINE GEOMETRICO*

Outwardly, *Ethics takes* the form of a treatise on geometry. The title says it all: *Ethica ordine geometrico demonstrata*, "ethics demonstrated in the manner of geometers". Neither prudential advice nor authoritative arguments from a "master of wisdom", the *Ethics* aims to produce true knowledge, with a truth as indisputable as that of mathematical theorems.

The Best Part of Ourselves

The fundamental definitions on which Spinoza's philosophy is based are given in the opening pages of the *Ethics*. These definitions, abrupt, difficult and resistant to any beginner's introduction to Spinoza, seem to resist explanation. They are:

- The **cause of itself** (*causa sui*) as that which by its nature must exist or necessarily exists.

- **Substance** as that which is conceived by itself and not by means of another.

- The **attribute** as what the intellect perceives of the substance as constitutive of itself.

- The **mode**, i.e. the affections of the substance.

These basic definitions, which Spinoza completes as the *Ethics* progresses, are not metaphysical postulates, intuitions of being or revelations. They are acts of the intellect, or *intelligentia*: "By [X] I understand" (*intelligo*), Spinoza repeats.

Spinoza defines intelligence as "the best part of ourselves" (E4A chap. XXXII). Spinoza goes on to say: "There is therefore no rational life without intelligence, and things are good only insofar as they help man to enjoy the life of the spirit (*mentis vita*), which is defined by intelligence. Those, on the contrary, which prevent man from perfecting his Reason and enjoying a reasonable life, we say are bad" (*ibid.*, chap. V).

It is precisely because men possess this intelligence that the society of men is the best for us: "Apart from men, we know of nothing in Nature (*nihil singulare*) that can give us pleasure through the mind, and to which we can bind ourselves by friendship or some kind of social relationship. And consequently, what is found in Nature (*rerum natura*) apart from men, the norm (*ratio*) of our utility does not require us to conserve it, but advises us to keep it for various uses, to destroy it, or to adapt it by all means to our use" (*ibid.*, chap. XXVI).

Intelligence is the "life of the spirit", a life nourished by relationships with other men. And "it is above all useful to perfect the understanding, in other words Reason, as far as we can, and in this alone consists the sovereign felicity or beatitude of man. [...] This is why the ultimate end of the man who is led by Reason, that is, the supreme desire, which enables him to regulate, is that which leads him to adequately conceive himself, and all the things that can fall under his intelligence (*sub ipsius intelligentiami*)" (*ibid.*, chap. IV).

The Power of Nature

The starting point of Spinoza's thought: in the beginning is the eternal and infinite absolute, and this absolute is called "substance".

First of all, Spinoza turns the notion of infinity on its head. In his *Treatise on the Reform of the Understanding*, he argues that, since we know spontaneously through the imagination and not according to the real order of things, we assign the idea of infinity a negative connotation, which is given by the word itself: infinity is the non-finite. But this mode of knowledge reverses the real order. We must begin with the infinite without determination, precisely in order to move on to determination, which is negation: to determine is to establish a limit, in other words, to separate what is the determined thing from what it is not. Before we can think of anything finite, we have to think of the infinite (even if we can't imagine it). The difficulty lies in the fact that the

Chapter I: "On God" or the Nature of Things Demonstrated *ordine geometrico*

term infinite appears to be a negative term—since we cannot imagine the infinite, and only seem to know the infinite in potential, as Aristotle argued[1]. But for Spinoza, the finite can only be determined as the negation of the infinite. The infinite is given first because it is absolutely without determination.

We could say that the finite emerges against a background of infinity. Some theologians say that God creates the world by withdrawing. It's a bit the same here: the entities of which the world is composed—finite entities in generally finite numbers—are cut-outs, as with a cookie-cutter, i.e. limitations of extent within extent, if we consider things under the attribute of extent. For example, a sphere is a "piece" of extent cut out by the rotation of a semicircle around its diameter. A finite thing is a determined thing, i.e. one to which a limit has been set: beyond this limit, the thing is no more. Determination is therefore negation.

This interpretation of the general meaning of infinity is undoubtedly debatable, as is any interpretation. But we must now try to support it by returning to the text of the *Ethics*. From the definitions to the first sixteen propositions, we shall gradually enter into the light of this absolute beginning.

---

1. Natural numbers are typically, for Aristotle and the Aristotelians, a kind of infinity in potential. We can never embrace the infinite set of natural numbers by thought, but we only know that whatever number n *is* as big as we want it to be, we can always find a number $n + 1$ bigger than it.

Absolute Beginning or Self-Cause

Spinoza's approach must be followed, since it's best to take his intentions seriously. *Ordine geometrico*: the *Ethics* has an internal logic, and we might as well start by following it, and begin at the beginning, i.e. at the start of the first part.

The beginning is the cause. But the cause is always caused by something else. So it is not the beginning. So we must look for the first cause, which is not caused by something else, and is therefore the cause of itself and of everything that follows. This is the "cause of itself" (*causa sui*).

> *D1. By self-cause, I mean that whose essence envelops existence, in other words that whose nature can only be conceived as existing.*

Some formidable words. "I hear" (*intelligo*): definitions are not revelations but acts of the intellect ("the best part of ourselves"). "I hear" simply means "I understand". These definitions must be absolutely rigorous and avoid any confusion (according to Spinoza, it is the confusion of words that is the essential source of errors and disputes, see Part II). So the cause of itself is "that whose essence envelops existence", or "that whose nature can only be conceived as existing". Essence and nature are practically synonyms here. To know the essence of a thing is to say what it is: the essence of a triangle is to be a three-sided figure. The essence of a man is to be an animal endowed with reason, and so on. The essence of a thing corresponds to the definition of the word that designates it (its meaning). To say of a thing that its essence encompasses existence is to say that existence is a property of that thing, a property without which the thing cannot be conceived. It all sounds very abstract, and possibly very confusing, but this first definition seems to refer to a great classic: the "ontological proof of the existence of God", a proof formulated by Saint Anselm of Canterbury and taken up by Descartes. The proof consists of a few propositions: 1) We have the idea of a perfect being, i.e. we know its essence. 2) A perfect being is one that possesses all perfections. 3) Without being able to enumerate all the perfections (which must be infinite in number), we immediately see that existence is such a perfection. (An infinitely good, existing being is clearly superior to an infinitely good, non-existent being!) 4) Conclusion: from our knowledge of the idea of perfect being, we therefore necessarily derive its existence. 5) God is an absolutely perfect being, so God exists!

This reasoning gives the impression of being pure sophistry, and indeed Descartes, who must have sensed this, sought and expounded other proofs of God's existence. Kant will show that this "proof" is flawed at the root, and that the same is true of all proofs of God's existence: existence is not the predicate of any thing, he asserts, and there is no more a predicate in a truly existing thing than in a merely possible thing. Kant's complex reflection on the subject would take us too far. Let's just say that, for Kant, the existence of a thing is given in sensible perception, and so existence is not a logical question that pure theoretical reason could determine, but an extra-logical question. But in truth, Spinoza is not at all committed to any of these innumerable proofs of God's existence.

If the allusion to "ontological proof" is transparent in this first definition, Spinoza is doing something quite different. It's not a question of asserting that "God exists", but of laying the foundations that make rigorous philosophical thought possible. Moreover, Spinoza does not say "there is a cause of itself, and it is God"; he merely defines the cause of itself. He does not posit the existence of a "self-cause", but only the logical necessity, the inflexible necessity of thought, of thinking such a "self-cause", and starting from there. The problem for Spinoza—we'll come back to this later—is not whether our thinking corresponds to a reality outside our thinking—in this case, whether this "self-cause" I'm talking about actually exists. The problem is to ensure the logical coherence of thought, to establish the right order of thought production.

However, before moving on to the next definition, we know, or at least are beginning to know, not what the cause of itself really is, but how we should order our thoughts. Nevertheless, we don't know what cause is in general. But we'll come back to that later.

Chapter I: "On God" or the Nature of Things Demonstrated *ordine geometrico*

The Finite as Determination of the Infinite: Finite in its Kind

We've already said it: in the *Ethics*, Spinoza doesn't first define the infinite, but the finite. If he doesn't define the infinite, it's perhaps simply because it doesn't need to be defined and, more importantly, doesn't even have to be defined—a defined infinite would be a funny thing. This definition of the finite is clear enough:

> *D2. A thing is said to be finite in its kind if it can be limited by another thing of the same kind. For example, a body is said to be finite because we can always conceive of a larger one. Similarly, a thought is limited by another thought. But a body is not limited by a thought, nor a thought by a body.*

So there is no such thing as an absolutely finite thing, only things that are finite in their kind. The finite is always relative to a kind of thing. This means that there are many kinds of things. Spinoza gives two examples: bodies and thoughts. An amoeba, a table, a horse or the Moon can be perceived as bodies, i.e. extended things. What these very different bodies have in common is only that they occupy a certain portion of space, and that they can be fully determined once their measurements and position have been determined. Why is a body finite in its kind? Spinoza gives a simple answer: because I can always conceive of a larger one. If I say, for example, that the universe—our visible universe—"measures" fifteen billion light-years, it's still finite, since I can conceive of a universe of fifteen billion light-years plus one! Or to put it another way: a body is finite because I can always conceive of another body alongside it, so that together they form a larger body[2].

The second example is things like "thinking". There are all kinds of very different thoughts: the thought that "2 + 2 = 4" or that "the sum of the three angles of a triangle is two rights", the thought that "I hate spinach" or the thought that "the cat is on the rug", and many others. A thought is "finite in its kind", Spinoza tells us, but he doesn't give us an illustration to help us grasp what a finite thought is. The difference between Spinoza's example and our examples of thought is obvious. We have notions of finite and infinite when it comes to numbers and quantities. The set of integers is infinite, because "it never stops", but every integer is finite, because no matter how big m is, there is always $n > m$ (e.g. $n = m + 1$). But these notions of number and measure don't apply to thoughts. Thoughts have no dimension or position, and cannot be ordered in relation to each other like numbers, at least not real numbers. The relation $>$ (or $<$) defines a total order for the reals (and integers): given two numbers x and y, we necessarily have either $x > y$,

---

2. The most widely accepted cosmological theories today admit that our universe is finite. This is not to say that we know its limits (because it would have no limits), but that we could conceive of a larger one, and that it is only empirical data that lead us to estimate it at thirteen billion nine hundred million light-years.

or $x = y$, or $y > x$. This is no longer true for complexes. This is no longer true of complex numbers. Complex numbers are "two-dimensional" numbers, with a real part and an imaginary part (by convention, i designates the imaginary number $(\sqrt{-1})$ or the number such that $i^2 = -1$). An imaginary number is therefore written $z = (a + bi)$. It's impossible to write that $(3 + 2i) > (2 + 2i)$. I can only compare complex numbers in terms of their "modulus" $\|z\| = (\sqrt{(a^2 + b^2)}$ or their "argument" $\theta = \arccos(b/a)$. Nevertheless, we have no trouble admitting that all these complex numbers are finite "of their kind". To a complex number $z1$ I can always add $z2$ and get a third complex $z3 = z1 + z2$.

However, we intuitively understand that a thought is finite and limited by another thought (we'll come back to this when it comes to establishing the nature of thought). For example, the thought "the weather is fine" is limited by the thought "it's raining", which negates it. Or: from two thoughts we can conceive a third. Or: one thought has a greater extension than the other (the concept of mammal has a greater extension than the concept of horse), and so on.

Finally, Spinoza clarifies the idea of "finitude in its kind" by saying that a body cannot limit a thought, nor a thought a body. If finiteness refers to the possibility of comparing, composing, placing side by side or delimiting, that goes without saying! My thought of a square one hundred kilometers square is no greater than that of a square one meter square. Nor is it smaller. It's the expression itself that's meaningless. A thought and a body have nothing in common: to be able to say that one thing can limit another, they must have something in common. For example, a fence delimits a field, because both are extended things. But there's nothing like that between thought and body, and we can see that these examples were not chosen by chance. As we shall see, if a thought cannot limit a body, nor a body limit a thought, then a body cannot determine a thought, nor a thought determine a body. Bodies and thoughts have nothing to do with each other! If I call the totality of bodies "matter" and the totality of thoughts "mind", then we see that neither matter determines mind nor mind determines matter, and therefore Spinoza is neither a materialist nor an idealist, in the common sense of these two terms.

The Real Itself or Substance

Substance is the key question of classical metaphysics. It plays a central role in Aristotle's philosophy, and in all the philosophy that derives from it, Scholasticism, against which Spinoza, like Descartes, will rise.

Let's look first at Spinoza's definition:

D3. By substance I mean that which is in itself and is conceived by itself, that is, that whose concept does not need the concept of another thing in order to be formed.

If we go back to Aristotle, we find a definition that has "a family resemblance": "Substance (*ousia*) is that which is properly said first and foremost; at the same time that which is not said of a certain subject and is not a certain subject; for example such a man or such a horse[3]."

Complex definition, difficult language. Let's try to understand it: what is properly said first and foremost is what is first said when we speak, and when we speak, we always speak of a given reality: "such and such a man", Peter or Paul. Then, when we talk about Peter or Paul, we talk about what is said about Paul (he's tall, he's young, etc.) or we attribute to him the fact of being a man, a reasonable animal. To cut a long story short, substance is first and foremost the individual grammatical subject (the one to whom we can attribute a proper noun). "Paul is great! Paul is subject and can only be subject of enunciation. I can't say that Peter is Paul in the same way as I say that Peter is tall. In short, Paul is a singular substance.

But Aristotle admits the word substance in another sense, what he calls second substance, genus and species. Paul's substance is what makes him Paul. But there's something that Peter and Paul have in common, and that makes them both human. And to make matters worse, it's not clear that *ousia* should be translated as "substance". Some translators translate *ousia* as "essence". Aristotle's *ousia* is not substance

---

3. Aristote, *Organon I*, « Catégories », chap. V.

in the common sense. It is not what stands underneath (*sub-stare),* even if we have become accustomed to translating the Greek οὐσία by the Latin *substantia* and by the French word "substance". What stands underneath for a Greek is *to hupokeimenon* translated by substratum or by sujet (what is *sub-jectum*) or even *hupostasis,* even if hypostasis takes on other meanings in Plotinus. *Ousia* is essence, that which makes a thing what it is, as a determinate thing, and not another thing.

In this sense, substance is both form and matter. The substrate, insofar as it is determined matter—the bronze from which the statue is made, to use Aristotle's famous example—is itself also a substance. This is not to say that the determined statue is a mere form, or a substance of substance. For Aristotle, there can be no substance of substance; the statue is bronze, but it is not *bronze.* The *ousia* of the statue is matter and form at the same time, in their unity; it is matter only insofar as it is delimited by its form, insofar as it has an edge, insofar as it cuts out clearly in space. This notion of delimitation immediately brings us back to another aspect of substance: substance is unity; it is not only what makes it be, but also what makes it *one.* Substance can take many forms, but in all cases, it never designates a thing, a matter; it is a category of thought.

For Aristotle, substance is a subtle notion, with multiple extensions, whose precise understanding raises major difficulties. Its elucidation is the essential purpose of the *Metaphysics.*

But this elucidation sometimes leads to dead ends. Aristotle turns the word over and over, illuminating its many facets and listing its various meanings. It has an ontological meaning; it designates a kind of thickness of what is; it shows its continuity and order. But it also has a logical meaning. This generalized substantialism becomes "substan-tivation": every fact in the world corresponds, ultimately, to a conceptual entity. The world is described entirely by names. There is not one substance, but as many substances as there are different realities designated by different names. Let's leave this Aristotelian definition of substance for a moment, and focus on the word itself. Substance (*substantia*) is what lies beneath (*sub-stare*). "Underneath" "Paul is tall", "Paul is sad", "Paul plays chess"—in short, underneath everything we can say about Paul—there is something constant, independent of ways of being and accidents: the substance Paul.

This, in a nutshell, is the "category" Spinoza inherits. Let's be clear: categories are the elementary terms of thought, just as nouns, verbs and adjectives are the elementary terms of spoken or written discourse. This distinction, which we introduce here between elements of thought and elements of discourse, is never clearly established in Aristotle, for whom thought and discourse are strictly equivalent—spoken words are symbols of thoughts, and written words are symbols of spoken words. We could say that substance is that which is designated by a noun, i.e. a name, a proper name for the individual substance, a common name for the second substance. In any case, Spinoza is now going to give substance a strange treatment. Substance, he says, is "that which is in itself" and not in something else. For example, whiteness is not a substance, because it is never "in itself", but always in something else: a white sheet, white snow, and so on. But Spinoza adds that substance is that whose concept does not need the concept of another thing to be formed. At first glance, this definition conforms to the Aristotelian-Scholastic canon, but the rest is less so. What can a concept be that doesn't need the concept of something else to be formed? Apparently, all concepts need other concepts to be formed. For example, the concept of cat to be formed may require the concept of mammal, feline, claws, moustache, sneakiness, and so on. I can imagine a cat if I've seen a cat, black and gaunt, crossing the street and been told, "There's a cat." But if, afterwards, I see a plump, white, purring Angora cat, I'll call it a "cat" because I've formed a concept of the cat, I can conceive of the cat in general, that is, I'm able to describe the "cat" essence, the "catness" of the cat. And for this operation, I need other words, other thoughts, other concepts. At first glance, then, it seems that concepts are like words in a dictionary: to define words, you need other words, and it's a kind of circle. To build concepts, you need other concepts.

So what can a thing be whose concept needs no other concepts to be formed? It can't be a particular "being"—dog, cat, earth, iron, water, air. None of these. What needs no other concepts to be formed is simply what we call "what is". The Greek philosophers, Parmenides for example, spoke

Chapter I: "On God" or the Nature of Things Demonstrated ordine geometrico

of "Being" and, of Being, Parmenides said that only one thing can be said of it: "Being is, non-being is not." To get a clearer idea of what Spinoza is saying, we need to go back to the biblical tradition—we must never forget that Spinoza is a Jew, a heretic to be sure, but a Jew, and that he studied to become a rabbi. When Moses asks God how he should refer to him when speaking to his people, God replies (in the Greek translation of the *Septuagint*), *egô eimi ho ôn*, which the Latin translation (the *Vulgate*) renders as *ego sum qui sum*, "I am who I am" (Exodus, 3). And God adds: "This is what you will answer the Israelites: he who calls himself 'I am' has sent me to you." God calls himself "I am". God has no face, no name other than "I am"; he is eternal and infinite, and can be conceived of by himself, without the need for the concept of something else, since that would be to deny his eternity and infinity. We'll continue along this path a little further on. Substance is therefore anything but a singular entity, as in Aristotle's case; on the contrary, it is the absolutely indeterminate, the absolute basis of all being and thought.

What We Perceive of Reality: Attributes

A little more difficult still, here's the attribute:

D4. By attribute, I mean what the understanding perceives of the substance as constituting its essence.

This notion of attribute raises many questions, and Spinoza gives only scattered indications on the subject. The attribute is what the understanding perceives: it could therefore be something that does not belong to the substance itself, but only to the way our understanding perceives the substance. But this interpretation is not the right one, and would take us away from the Spinozist conception of knowledge. There's a word that will put us on the right track in Definition VI. So let's wait a little longer to clarify this category of attribute. In a letter to Simon De Vries (*Letter 9*), Spinoza clarifies: "By substance, I mean that which is in itself and is conceived by itself; that is, that whose concept does not imply the concept of another thing. It is the same thing that I mean by attribute, except that this term is used from the point of view of the understanding which attributes to the substance such and such a determined nature."

In short, attribute and substance are the same thing, but substance is expressed in attributes insofar as it is considered not in itself, but insofar as the mind thinks it. The more a substance exists, the more attributes it has, and an infinite substance will therefore have an infinite number of attributes (*ibid.*).

Chapter I: "On God" or the Nature of Things Demonstrated ordine geometrico

Ways of Being, or Mode

The mode, which could also be called "manner" as some translations do, begins to take us into the complexity of the world.

D5. By mode I mean the affections of substance, in other words that which is in something else, by which it is also conceived.

Substance is therefore affected, i.e. modified (which is why the translation "mode" is still preferable). The mode is a reality, not a reality that exists by itself, but only in something else. For example, a hole is indeed a certain kind of reality; when Gruyère cheese is finished, the fermentation of the dough has produced air bubbles that make Gruyère a cheese with holes. Holes are not "nothing". If Gruyère no longer has holes, it's no longer Gruyère but, for example, Comté. The hole in Gruyère is indeed an "affection" of the paste from which the cheese is made. But the hole exists only in the cheese, i.e. "in something else", and so doesn't exist by itself. And the hole in Gruyère cheese can only be conceived of if we possess the concept of Gruyère cheese. For the theory of general relativity, masses are merely points around which space-time curves. A star, a planet or a black hole are merely modifications of space-time. Mode, or manner, is simply a particular way of being, determined by substance.

God, in Other Words, Reality in its Totality

The definition of God comes sixth. The first part is entitled *De Deo* ("On God"), yet it doesn't begin with God. There is a definition here, and a demonstration of his existence, but located later in the text. Let's look at the definition:

D6. By God, I mean an absolutely infinite being, i.e. a substance consisting of an infinite number of attributes, each of which expresses an eternal and infinite essence.

We have to start with a definition. Indeed, to ask whether God exists or not, when we don't know what it is, is a futile enterprise. Before answering the question: "Do you believe in God?", we must always begin by answering: "What do you mean by this word?". We can also see how the definition of God is composed from the preceding definitions: God is a substance, he is "absolutely infinite" (so not "finite in kind") and he "consists in an infinity of attributes". So we have confirmation that substance and being are the same thing: a substance is a being. An infinite substance is an infinite being. Next, Spinoza says that a substance "consists" of attributes. Attributes are part of the essence of substance. If the mind perceives certain attributes, it perceives, in a certain respect, the essence of the substance, since the attribute and the substance, as we saw above, are more or less the same thing, except that the attribute is the substance perceived by the

Chapter I: "On God" or the Nature of Things Demonstrated *ordine geometrico*

understanding. Finally, as we know that the more attributes a substance has, the more it exists, an absolutely eternal and infinite substance exists absolutely, and so it "consists" of an "infinity of attributes", and these attributes "express" an eternal and infinite essence. This means that when the mind grasps an attribute, it perceives an eternal and infinite essence, but obviously only under a single attribute. To perceive the universe as eternal and infinite, as Giordano Bruno and Galileo did, is to perceive God (or the eternal and infinite substance) under the attribute of extent.

The definition is supplemented by an explanation, as this is obviously a crucial point, and no equivocation can be allowed to remain. Firstly, Spinoza contrasts the absolutely infinite with the infinite in its kind. We've heard of the "finite in its kind", and here we have the "infinite in its kind". For example, for a mathematician, a straight line is infinite in its kind, but it is not absolutely infinite, since it has a limit (it is delimited by two points or by the intersection of two planes). The same applies to the plane, to three-dimensional space, to the set of whole or real numbers, and so on. But if there is an infinite absolute being, then everything that expresses an essence and has no negation belongs to it! It's important to note that we can't say much more than this, because to do so would be to begin to determine it, and thus deny its absolute infinity.

The verb "to express" plays an important role (as Gilles Deleuze clearly demonstrated in his *Spinoza et le problème de l'expression*, Éditions de Minuit, 1968). What does "express" mean? Let's leave etymology aside for a moment: to express is to obtain juice by pressure. When we express something in words, we're giving voice to something that previously couldn't be heard. Music can express feelings, etc. Expression makes present, visible or audible what was compressed. In what sense does the attribute express substance? In that it makes manifest, for the understanding, the essence of substance. If substance is eternal and infinite, then each attribute naturally expresses an eternal and infinite essence; each attribute is thought of as eternal and infinite (e.g. nature).

A Free Thing: A Paradoxical Definition of Freedom

D7. A thing is said to be free when it exists according to the sole necessity of its nature and is determined by itself alone to act. On the contrary, a thing is called necessary, or rather constrained, when it is determined by another to exist and produce an effect according to a definite and determined reason.

This definition sets up the essential problematic of *Ethics* as it deals with the rules to be followed to achieve bliss, i.e. the *summum bonum*. It's a seemingly paradoxical definition of freedom, but one whose power can be measured in Parts IV

Chapter I: "On God" or the Nature of Things Demonstrated *ordine geometrico*

and V of the work. To be free is not to "do as you please", to go indifferently to right or left, or to be able to say "no" when saying "yes" is required. The freedom to act badly or destroy oneself is not freedom at all for Spinoza. To be free is first and foremost to be determined to exist by the mere necessity of one's nature. There are few finite things that can be said to be determined to exist by the mere necessity of their nature: a man is determined to exist by the procreative action of his parents! He is not free, because he is caused by something else. In this sense, that which is self-caused is a free thing, since its essence envelops its existence—it exists by the mere necessity of its nature. And so anything that is not self-caused is not free. In this way, finite things are produced by infinite series of causes and effects—series that our understanding cannot fully embrace, because it is far too limited. The expression can be understood in a more restricted sense: to exist by its own nature, and to be determined by itself alone to act, is quite simply to act in accordance with the principle of conservation of one's own existence (cf. part III): each thing insofar as it exists tends to give its existence the maximum possible. To be constrained, on the other hand, is to be determined by another to exist and act according to the actions we undergo.

Eternity or Existence Itself

To conclude these definitions in Part I, here's the key term in Spinozist philosophy: eternity. We come across this term again in Part V, when Spinoza makes the startling statement that "We feel and experience that we are eternal" (E5P23S).

D8. By eternity, I mean existence itself, insofar as it is conceived as necessarily following from the sole definition of an eternal thing.

Therefore, the existence of a thing is eternal when this existence derives from the sole definition of the thing. *Strictly speaking,* to be eternal is to be "self-caused". For there to be a beginning and an end, i.e. for a temporal order to be introduced, there must be a cause that determines the thing to exist and a cause that determines it to cease to exist, and so the thing is no longer "cause of itself".

That might sound a little narrow and abstract. In fact, it's about something other than precise explanation. The existence that follows from the definition of an eternal thing is conceived as "eternal truth", and such truth is only that which can be explained neither by duration nor by time (even if that duration is indefinite). Eternity is therefore not to be confused with immortality.

Logical Axioms Define the Structure of Reality

These axioms are a kind of logical principle that we must follow in order to arrive at a true knowledge of the nature of things. The first two, which are closely related, seem to take up the distinction between substance (that which is in itself, and is conceived by itself) and mode (that which is in something else, and can only be conceived by something else). Here, Spinoza takes a more general standpoint, setting out the principle of the excluded third from a particular angle.

A1. Everything that is, is either in itself, or in something else.

One is tempted to add that Monsieur de la Palice would have said as much! The next one seems to say the same thing differently:

A2. What cannot be conceived by something else must be conceived by itself.

We must emphasize the parallelism that systematically links being and thinking, as if they were one and the same[4]: "being" and "being conceived" go together, and the pair "in itself/in something else" is matched by the pair "by itself/by

---

4. Parmenides maintained that thinking and being are the same thing.

something else". Beyond the apparent obvious (but an axiom must obviously be true!), it's a question of opposing what is in itself (substance) and what is "in something else" (affections). And the alternative means that knowledge can only concern the substance or the affections (or modifications) of the substance.

The following three axioms briefly explain the principle of causality.

A3. From a given determinate cause, an effect necessarily follows, and on the contrary, if there is no determinate cause, it is impossible for an effect to follow.

All things proceed from the relationship between cause and effect. A cause produces effects (necessarily), and without a cause, there is no effect! Note that Spinoza is careful not to formulate things the other way round (e.g., from effects to causes). In this axiom, causality always goes from causes to effects. There are powerful reasons for this, to which we'll return later.

Spinoza continues the parallelism between reality and knowledge. If causes produce effects, then knowledge of effects depends on knowledge of causes. This is why all true knowledge is knowledge of causes.

A4. Knowledge of the effect depends on knowledge of the cause and the envelope.

Note that knowledge of the effect "envelops" knowledge of the cause, i.e. knowledge of the effect necessarily includes knowledge of the cause. Knowledge is therefore knowledge of the production process. For example, to know what a circle is is to know that it is generated by the rotation of a radius around a fixed point.

A5. Nor can things that have nothing in common with each other be understood by each other; in other words, the concept of one does not envelop the concept of the other.

This axiom formulates the same thesis as the previous one in a different way. If two things have nothing in common, then one cannot be the cause of the other, or both cannot be understood as the effects of a common cause.

A6. A true idea must match the object it represents.

Another seemingly banal axiom. The true idea agrees with its ideate: this seems to repeat the classical thesis that truth is the adequacy of thing and thought. But that would be reading too quickly. Spinoza is not saying that truth lies in the adequacy of mind and things (*adequatio rei et intellectus*), but that the true idea must agree with its ideate. It simply states that the true idea (as it exists objectively in the mind) must represent what is in nature. But this tells us nothing about the process by which a true idea is formed. Nor does it tell us how an idea can "represent" a thing.

A7. For what can be conceived as non-existent, essence does not envelop existence.

This seems to follow from the definitions, particularly that of self-cause. This axiom could be the contraposition of definition I.

The Rational Construction of God, a God without Transcendence

Having laid these initial foundations for any geometrical demonstration, Spinoza goes on to derive propositions, i.e. demonstrable assertions, assertions whose truth must be indubitable. We're starting down a very abstract path, where Spinoza formulates very general propositions whose content and scope are not immediately obvious.

E1P1. Substance is inherently prior to its affections.

"This is obvious from definitions 3 and 5," says the demonstration. Indeed, affections are affections of substance, and so substance is indeed first.

Chapter I: "On God" or the Nature of Things Demonstrated *ordine geometrico*

E1P2. Two substances with different attributes have nothing in common.

This is "obvious from definition 3", says Spinoza. Each substance must exist in itself and be conceived of by itself. So the concept of one does not envelop the concept of the other. We could make this demonstration more precise: since attributes express substance, if two substances have different attributes, they therefore have different essences.

E1P3. If things have nothing in common, one cannot be the cause of the other.

If we combine proposition II with axioms IV and V, we have an obvious demonstration.

E1P4. Two or more distinct things are distinguished from each other either by the diversity of the attributes of the substances, or by the diversity of the affections of these substances.

This follows from the fact that there is nothing outside the understanding except substances and their affections. So things can only be distinguished by one or the other.

E1P5. In nature, there cannot be two or more substances of the same nature or attribute.

This is where we get to the heart of the matter, i.e. the demonstration that there is only one eternal and infinite substance, which is God!

Let's try to clarify the demonstration. As is often the case, Spinoza uses a demonstration by the absurd.

- Suppose there are several distinct substances, they can be distinguished either according to their attributes or according to their affections (by virtue of P4).

- If this is according to their attributes, there is only one substance with the same attribute. Since the attribute expresses the essence of the substance, two substances with the same attribute would have the same essence, making them one and the same substance.

- If it is according to their affections, as the substance is prior to its affections, we can put aside the affections and see that two substances cannot be distinguished according to their affections. The diversity of affections gives us no information about the substance, since they are posterior to it. So it's not because affections are multiple that there are several substances, and it's not affections that enable us to distinguish between several substances. Now, neither the diversity of attributes nor that of affections allows us to distinguish several substances, whereas they could only be distinguished on the basis of attributes or affections. Therefore, there is only one substance: C.Q.F.D.

E1P6. A substance cannot be produced by another substance.

If there are two distinct substances, they have nothing in common. On the contrary, the relationship of cause and effect presupposes that they have something in common (the idea of the effect envelops the idea of the cause). C.Q.F.D.!

From this Spinoza draws a corollary:

E1P6C. From this it follows that a substance cannot be produced by anything else. For in nature there is nothing apart from substances and their affections, as is evident from axiom I and definitions 3 and 5. Now, one substance cannot be produced by another (according to the preceding proposition). So, absolutely speaking, a substance cannot be produced by something else.

The corollary is an extension of the proposition: if, according to P6, one substance cannot be produced by another, *a fortiori*, it cannot be produced by anything else. Therefore, it is unique, eternal and self-caused.

We'll now follow all the almost obvious consequences of what we've just demonstrated.

E1P7. It is in the nature of the substance to exist.

Since a substance cannot be produced by another, it is not caused by anything else, so it is self-caused and according to D1 it is in the nature of a self-cause to exist.

E1P8. All substance is necessarily infinite.

Here again, a demonstration by the absurd is required. If a substance is finite, this means that it is limited by another substance of the same nature or attribute. Now, according to P5, there cannot be two substances of the same nature or attribute, so the substance is infinite, and therefore unique.

Tentative conclusion: a substance exists and it is infinite!

Proposition VIII is followed by two scolies that deserve a closer look.

Scholia I (E1P8S1) notes that Proposition VII alone implies the infinite character of substance. The finite, Spinoza reminds us, envelops a negation (see the definition of "finite in its kind"). Infinity, on the other hand, is the absolute affirmation of existence. So, to assert that substance exists by nature is to assert its absolute existence, and therefore its infinity.

Scholia II (E1P8S2) is clearly polemical. He attacks those who "do not distinguish between modifications of substances and substances themselves, and do not know how things happen." And Spinoza goes on to list all manner of fables that such people believe because they imagine things instead of understanding them in their order of production. Now, to confuse substance with its modes is to confuse, for example, human nature with divine nature, and thus to attribute human feelings to God. This is the beginning of a critique that will continue until the appendix to Part I.

This scolie recalls the definition of substance ("that which is in itself is conceived by itself") and argues that

Proposition VII should be held as an axiom or "common notion". This is the first appearance of the "common notion", which plays a central role in the possibility of moving beyond knowledge by imagination to rational knowledge (see explanation in Part II). The scolie thus clarifies the modes/substance distinction. If I have a true idea of substance, this true idea includes the existence of substance. On the other hand, I can have a true idea of a modification without this modification existing, since modifications can exist only in the understanding, whereas substance exists in itself. To try and grasp what we're talking about, let's take an example. I can conceive of a house that conforms to the laws of physics, the strength of materials and my desires, but I can't conceive that reality doesn't exist! Spinoza takes a very particular example: "If, then, someone were to say that he has a clear and distinct, i.e. true, idea of a substance, and yet doubts whether it exists, it would in truth be as if he were to say that he has a true idea and yet does not know whether it is false or true."

To have a true idea is to know that one has a true idea, and not to doubt it. Indirectly, Spinoza refutes the Cartesian conception of truth as a "clear and distinct idea". We'll come back to this later. From all this, it follows that substance cannot be created. It is therefore uncreated. But to these demonstrations by the absurd, Spinoza adds another, slightly more subtle but of the utmost importance, to show that there can only be one substance of the same nature.

1° That the true definition of each thing envelops and expresses only the nature of the thing defined. From which it follows:

2° That no definition envelops and expresses any determined number of individuals, since it expresses nothing other than the nature of the thing defined. For example, the definition of a triangle expresses nothing other than the simple nature of the triangle, but not a given number of triangles.

3° It should be noted that, for every existing thing, there is necessarily a determined cause that makes it exist.

4° Finally, it should be noted that this cause by which a given thing exists must either be contained in the very nature and definition of the existing thing (because, indeed, it belongs to its nature to exist), or exist outside it.

Suppose there are twenty men in nature. We need to explain why there are twenty, and no more and no less. But this explanation is not contained in human nature (the definition of man does not include the fact that there are only twenty!). Consequently, the cause must be sought elsewhere. The cause of each of them must be explained. Conversely, since a substance exists in and of itself, and since its definition encompasses its existence, there cannot be several substances of the same nature (otherwise there would be no cause for this multiplicity). What Spinoza is questioning here is the possibility of there being several absolutely identical things, differing only in number. In truth, no two things can be

Chapter I: "On God" or the Nature of Things Demonstrated *ordine geometrico*

absolutely identical, and therefore only singular things exist. Here again, metaphysics prepares the theory of knowledge, as we shall see in Part II.

E1P9. The more reality or being a thing possesses, the more attributes belong to it.

This proposition follows from definition IV, says the laconic demonstration. It implies that there are degrees of reality or being. Substance is that which possesses the absolute degree of being, and it is for this reason that it is uncreated and therefore eternal. And so, the more attributes a thing has, the more it expresses substance, and therefore the more reality it has.

E1P10. Every attribute of a substance must be self-designed.

This follows from the definition of substance. Substance exists per se and must be conceived per se, and as the attribute expresses for the understanding the essence of the substance, so must it. The scolie develops this point by showing that distinct attributes of the same substance do not form two distinct realities, but explain this same reality in two distinct and unrelated ways.

E1P11. God, in other words a substance made up of an infinite number of attributes, each of which expresses an eternal and infinite essence, necessarily exists.

An important proposition, followed by three demonstrations and a long scolie. The first demonstration by the absurd is lapidary. It boils down to the idea that it is impossible to conceive of the non-existence of a substance made up of an infinite number of attributes—in other words, it is impossible for reality not to exist. The other demonstrations remain at a very high level of abstraction. Here, it makes more sense to try and grasp what we're talking about, because the name "God" can obviously mislead those who identify God with a person, or with three persons in one, for example. Since there are only substances or affections in nature, and there can only be one substance, all affections are affections of that substance. Put another way, everything that is in God can only be conceived by God. Spinoza's God, it is sometimes said, is the "great whole", and Spinoza is described as a "pantheist". But this is not exactly the case. There is no trace of "mysticism", God appears as a logical construct: God is simply reality in all its dimensions (or attributes). And reality is eternal, because it is impossible to assign temporal limits and temporal evolution to it. Affections (modes) can be born and disappear, but this birth and disappearance presuppose the eternity of reality. It is infinite for similar reasons. If we think of a finite reality, then implicitly we think of a beyond this finite reality—without which it would be impossible to think of its finitude. When we say that the universe is finite and give its size, we are not referring to the universe as such, but only to the physical universe we can observe and understand today

Chapter I: "On God" or the Nature of Things Demonstrated ordine geometrico

according to the laws of physics we have mastered. But that doesn't mean that reality isn't infinite. In short, for Spinoza—and for us!—it's impossible not to start from the absolute of eternal, infinite reality, which can be explained (or expressed) in an infinite number of attributes.

Antonio Crivotti, an Italian philosopher, has given an interpretation of Spinoza using the methods of modern logical analysis. He shows that, however one conceives of "God" and "existence", the Spinozist construction necessarily led to attributing the property "existence" to the entity "God" (see on this point http://denis-collin.viabloga.com/news/spinoza-et-l-atheisme). Crivotti's thesis is that the construction of God in the first eleven propositions of the *Ethics* is motivated above all by the desire to escape the accusation of atheism.

Hegel held a radically opposite view. In his *Lessons on the History of Philosophy*, he refutes Spinoza's accusation of atheism, saying that his system could just as well be characterized as acosmism. Since atheists deny God and leave only the world, it could be said of Spinoza that he denies the world and leaves only God, since all that is cannot be and cannot be conceived outside of God.

E1P12. In truth, we cannot conceive of any attribute of a substance from which it would follow that the substance can be divided.

This proposal is supplemented by the following:

E1P13. The infinite absolute substance is indivisible.

And above all the corollary:

E1P13C. Hence it follows that no substance, and consequently no corporeal substance, insofar as it is a substance, is divisible.

These three propositions establish the nature of infinity for Spinoza. Infinity is indivisible, because if we could divide infinity, it would no longer be infinite, or we would have two infinities, which is impossible. The uniqueness of substance and its infinity are two aspects of the same idea.

E1P14. Apart from God, no substance can be or be conceived.

Consequence of the above: there is no substance other than God. There is no such thing as an extended substance on the one hand, and a thinking substance on the other, as in Descartes. Bodily substance as such is indivisible: this means that, for Spinoza, there is no void (as for Descartes), not because Spinoza imagines that there is invisible or swirling matter between visible bodies (e.g. between stars), but because, for him, physical reality is uniquely extended, i.e. fully conceptualizable by geometry. In reality, for Spinoza, as for Descartes, this remained a purely theoretical program. Newton's physical theory of the late seventeenth century

Chapter I: "On God" or the Nature of Things Demonstrated *ordine geometrico*

combines two heterogeneous elements: on the one hand, purely geometrical elements (a three-dimensional space, spatial relations between the bodies that populate this space), and on the other, purely physical elements, the masses of bodies. But in Newtonian physics, there is no necessary relationship between the two. It's only with Einstein that the program of geometrization of physics can be accomplished, once mass is considered as a curvature of space-time. Of course, we shouldn't make Spinoza a precursor of Einstein—even if Einstein claims that his God is Spinoza's God (see our article on Einstein's religion and Spinoza's: http://denis-collin.viabloga.com/news/dieu-ou-la-nature; and also Gustavo Cevolani's study, "Einstein and Spinoza": http://denis-collin.viabloga.com/news/einstein-et-spinoza). However, his meta-physical radicalism proved fruitful, and Einstein's scientific audacity is a good match for Spinoza's philosophical audacity.

Let us emphasize the two corollaries of Proposition XIV:

E1P14C1. It follows very clearly from there:

1° That God is unique, i.e. (according to definition 6) that in nature there is only one substance, and that it is absolutely infinite, as we have already indicated in the scolie of proposition 10.

E1P14C2. It follows:

2° That the extended thing and the thinking thing are attributes of God or (according to axiom I) affections of the attributes of God.

In nature, there is only one substance, God. Consequently, nature is made up of... God, and so God and nature are one and the same thing. God is nature (Spinozist materialists prefer). Nature is God (others may prefer). In any case, the equivalence is strictly established. In other words, God's essence can be explained in terms of either extension or thought, without there being any relationship of dependence between one and the other.

Hence the following proposition:

E1P15. All that is, is in God, and nothing, without God, can neither be nor be conceived.

Once again, we note the parallel between being and being conceived. What is conceivable can be, and what is is conceivable. When Spinoza says that "nothing without God can either be or be conceived", we must take *conceive* in the two common senses of this word: the mind conceives ideas, the mother conceives a child. Ideas and things are produced by God in the same moment, and nothing can be conceived outside of God (which is why, a little further on, Spinoza affirms that God is the "immanent cause" of all things, not the "transitive cause" (P18).

Once we've reached this point, we'll see that the first part will take another direction. We'll be able to explore everything that follows from God's nature. But first, the long scolie that follows this proposition deserves our attention, as

Chapter I: "On God" or the Nature of Things Demonstrated *ordine geometrico*

it poses a whole series of difficult questions and constitutes a unity in itself.

The scolie (P15S) begins with a recurring theme: the denunciation of superstitious people who imagine God as a man. This anthropomorphic vision of God is the furthest thing from true knowledge. But it is also a question of discussing the classical dualist position which, while recognizing on the one hand that God—being an infinite Being—cannot take the form of a figure, at the same time completely sets aside corporeal nature, which "they consider to have been created by God". This is impossible, since one substance cannot create another! Spinoza extends this demonstration, however, by specifically refuting two kinds of argument:

- First of all, the advocates of a transcendent God reserve the infinite character for him, whereas the corporeal substance (or expanse), according to them, cannot be infinite, but is only, at most, indefinite. Here, Spinoza comes face to face with the well-known paradoxes used by those who refuse to consider the infinite in act. Here's a simplified version that sums them all up: whole numbers are infinite in number, and so are even numbers. But there are two integers for an even number, so we'd have to assume an infinity double another.

- Next, a more theological argument: corporeal substance, being divisible into parts, is passive, and therefore cannot belong to the divine essence.

Spinoza responds to the first argument in several stages. If we accept Spinoza's answer to the first argument—that infinity is rationally thinkable—the objections to the second fall *ipso facto*.

1) The absurdities exposed by those who refuse to consider the infinity of bodily substance derive solely from the fact that they assume "an infinite and measurable quantity composed of finite parts". An infinite, measurable quantity is indeed something as impossible as a square circle. Measurement presupposes the finite, and infinity is not a very large quantity, larger than any we can imagine. It is this absurdity that produces the other absurdities. But if we agree with Spinoza that corporeal substance can only be "conceived as infinite, unique and indivisible", then these absurdities disappear. Now, corporeal substance is no more composed of finite parts than the body is composed of surfaces, and surfaces of lines, and lines of points. Indeed, a non-zero quantity cannot be a sum of zeros, and in the same way, you can't compose a straight line with points—nor a duration with a succession of instants, as Bergson would say much later. Nor a surface with a sum of straight lines, etc. This "continuistic" conception of expanse obviously implies the denial of the existence of the void.

2) Spinoza then uses a second argument: if corporeal substance were made up of parts, one of these parts could be annihilated, and therefore the void could exist, which it says it doesn't! Here, he turns a Cartesian argument (the negation of the void, which is used to explain "whirling" movements) against Cartesian metaphysics. Of course, Pascal is going

Chapter I: "On God" or the Nature of Things Demonstrated ordine geometrico

to demonstrate that we are obliged to admit the void (see *Traité du vide*), so it may seem that Spinoza's argument here is really weak. But the truth is, it's not clear what the point of the argument is, and for that we need to move on to the next arguments.

3)   The third argument: we are inclined "by nature" to divide quantity. But quantity is only divisible in the abstract, by imagination, whereas substantially it is not. Considered by the understanding as substance, quantity is not divisible, but infinite, unique and indivisible. This means that there are two ways of considering quantity: either extensively (*partes extra partes*), or intensively as a whole. An extensive quantity is simply conceived as a summation of the magnitudes of the parts (for example, when I imagine the number 3 with the image of three logs, like those used by children to learn to count). On the contrary, an intensive magnitude is a magnitude considered in itself. Let's face it, the scolie passage on this question is singularly enigmatic[5].

4)   Apparently to illustrate and complete arguments (2) and (3), Spinoza argues that the inability to perceive these distinctions comes simply from confusing substance and affections. The affections of bodily substance do form parts that can be counted, but this division of affections does not mean a division of substance at all.

---

5. Aristotle, *Organon I*, "Categories", chap. V.

An Interpretation of Spinoza's Metaphysics

Spinoza's arguments deserve to be revisited and updated in the light of our scientific knowledge. For example, that there is no such thing as a vacuum, but only a state (an affection) of matter, is what standard physical theories admit today: the vacuum is a particular quantum state and not the absence of matter, since matter and energy are equivalent and the energy of the vacuum can be defined. Without even going into these subtleties, even classical physics (pre-quantum and pre-relativist if you like) has never considered the vacuum to be pure nothingness, since the vacuum has physical properties: electromagnetic waves propagate in it, it has conductance, magnetic permeability, etc. So there's no need to oppose matter and the vacuum, but only to see two different affections of the same bodily substance.

Similarly, Georg Cantor's theory of transfinite numbers provides an elegant solution to the paradoxes of infinity.

To get out of the paradoxes of infinity, Cantor starts from set theory. While philosophers and mathematicians refused to make infinity a number—in analysis, we write that "$x \to \infty$" (x tends to infinity) but never $x = \infty$!—Cantor introduced the number as the power or cardinal of a set. Finite sets are those with cardinal 0, 1, 2, 3... and other sets are called transfinite. The first transfinite set is the set of cardinals that we show cannot be finite. And this transfinite set is given the cardinal $\aleph_0$.

The notion of cardinal was defined by matching the elements of a set. Two sets A and B whose elements can be linked one to one have the same cardinal. A set of which a (strict) part can be put in bijection with the whole is a transfinite set. For example, the set of natural integers (N) is such a set, since if we call P the set of even numbers:

1) $P \subset N$ (Indeed, every even number is a natural number, but not every natural number is even).

2) There is a bijection between P and N ("one-to-one correspondence" says Cantor) since:

a. $\forall x \in N, \exists y \in P : y = 2x$

b. $\forall x \in P, \exists y \in N : y = x/2$

3) So P G N (or P and N have the same cardinal, which is $\aleph_0$).

The number $\aleph_0$ obviously behaves quite differently from ordinary finite numbers. For example, the following relationships can be verified:

- $\aleph_0 + 1 = \aleph_0$

- $2 . \aleph_0 = \aleph_0$

- If a is a number, a is transfinite, $\aleph_0 < a$

Cantor shows that every transfinite set has parts of cardinal $\aleph_0$ and, more generally, that every transfinite set has parts that are equivalent to it. This could provide an interpretation of the Spinozist proposition of the indivisibility of infinity: if half of a transfinite set is equivalent to the whole, then the set is not, strictly speaking, divisible (in any case, it is not divisible in the way we conceive of divisibility by imagination).

Having constructed $\aleph 0$ (what we'll call the cardinal of a countable infinite set), we show that there is an immediately superior transfinite number ($\aleph 1$) and that all transfinite numbers form an ordered set.

Let's leave Cantor there. It is enough to have shown that the impossibility of conceiving infinity stems solely from the fact that we use our imagination instead of our understanding. Cantor shows that we can rigorously think infinity, since we can even order transfinite numbers.

This is not to say that Cantor's physics or number theory are Spinozist. Scientific theory always has a certain autonomy from metaphysics. There is a dialectical relationship between physics and metaphysics: metaphysics provides intuitions that then allow physics to develop on its own, and physics, in turn, leads to new metaphysical questioning. In any case, autonomy does not at all mean independence and radical separation. Ordinary positivism in this field is invalidated as soon as we try to make something other than an operational science for technical purposes. If we try to interpret the results of theory in order to make sense of them, then we are engaging in metaphysics. By the same token, mathematics is not in itself a metaphysics, nor does it in itself provide such a metaphysics. Cantor is not "validating" Spinoza's philosophy, but simply giving an example of the kind of interpretation that can be drawn from Spinozist metaphysics.

God's Absolute Power

From Proposition XVI onwards, Spinoza unfolds all the consequences that can be drawn from the nature of God as just established. In all that follows, we must be careful not to forget this definition of God: an eternal and infinite substance made up of an infinite number of attributes, each of which expresses an eternal and infinite essence.

Spinoza will now consider God as a cause. God alone is a free cause, since he is the cause of himself and of all that can flow from him, and thus acts according to the necessity of his own nature. But the development that follows gives a very particular concept of this divine freedom. The scolie of proposition XVII is helpful in understanding what this is all about.

> *E1P17S. Others think that God is a free cause, because he can, according to them, cause those things which, as we have said, follow from his nature—that is, which are in his power—not to happen, in other words, not to be produced by him. But it's as if they were saying that God can make it so that, from the nature of the triangle, it does not follow that its three angles are equal to two rights; in other words, that from a given cause it does not follow the effect.*

The picture is set. Free does not mean arbitrary. "God is subtle but not malicious," said Einstein. God's freedom consists in doing everything that flows from his nature, but it cannot consist in not doing what flows from it. Everything in nature (and therefore in God's nature) is ordered according to a necessity that Spinoza clearly defines: a mathematical necessity. From the nature of the triangle, it follows that the sum of the three angles is worth two rights, and no one can make it worth three rights or one right, as circumstances dictate. As Einstein once said, "God doesn't play dice". For Spinoza, the affirmation of necessity is directed, on the one hand, against belief in miracles (God doesn't work miracles, he always acts according to the laws of his own nature) and, on the other hand, against those who invoke the "will of God", that asylum of ignorance: God obviously cannot have a will (since there could be no gap between his present state and a future state that he would "desire" as if it lacked something! More generally, moreover, there is no will in the strict sense—there is no difference between will and understanding.

This first criticism is coupled with a second, more radical one, which draws a real gulf between the God of religions or even of rationalist philosophers such as Descartes, Malebranche, etc., and Spinoza's God: "[...] neither will nor understanding belong to the nature of God".

Let's start with the first. "My opponents", says Spinoza, argue that they do not believe that God "can bring into existence anything of which he has actual knowledge". There is an infinity of possibilities in the divine understanding, but God only brings into being those he chooses by a decree of his

Chapter I: "On God" or the Nature of Things Demonstrated ordine geometrico

free will. For Spinoza, this conception is erroneous. In God, insofar as we understand him under the attribute of thought, exist an infinity of things in an infinity of modes and, by virtue of the parallelism between being and conceiving, everything that is conceived, everything of which there is an idea (provided it contains no contradiction), is necessarily called to come into being. And Spinoza, using a procedure he would employ again and again, shows that his opponents who claim to defend God's perfection by attributing to him a free will are in fact only restricting God's omnipotence. Omnipotence cannot be virtual; it must always be actual. Everything that is possible (i.e. an infinite number of things) must exist. But these possibilities cannot all exist at the same time under the attribute of extent. Some can only exist when others have disappeared, and finite beings that exist simultaneously can also collide and destroy each other. We'll return to this question later.

But above all, in this scolie, Spinoza denies that we can attribute will and understanding to God's nature. Either God's will and understanding can be attributed on the model of human will and understanding—but this is impossible without seriously transforming the true concept of the divine essence, as eternal and infinite—or God can be attributed something called divine understanding, but this is no longer properly speaking an understanding, since it must know things before they exist; in fact, this understanding is identified with God himself. The same applies to the will.

Once again, to attribute understanding and will to God is to conceive of God through the imagination as a kind of human.

E1P18. God is the immanent, but not transitive, cause of all things.

Since everything that is is in God and can only be conceived of by him, it goes without saying that God is the immanent cause of all things. All things exist because they are in God. A man may be the immediate cause of a thing's existence (for example, a man is the cause of another man's existence because he is his father), but he is not the cause of that man's essence, which is "in God", and therefore only a part of nature, whose course he follows. For Spinoza, then, there is no creation, procession or emanation. We're "on the plane of immanence", as Deleuze puts it. If God is the cause of A, which is the cause of B, etc., then God is the transitive cause of B. But in Spinoza, God is the immanent cause of A and B, because the essences of A and B are from all eternity in God. Moreover, if A is determined to produce B as an effect, A has been determined from all eternity to produce that effect. So God is the efficient cause of all things.

E1P19. God, in other words, all God's attributes are eternal.

This is a consequence of proposition XI. A "very obvious" proposition, says Spinoza, who recalls that he demonstrated

Chapter I: "On God" or the Nature of Things Demonstrated *ordine geometrico*

it differently in *Descartes' Principles of Philosophy*, proposition XIX of Part I. In this text, it is shown that we cannot think of limits to God's existence, otherwise we would have to conceive of perfect being as non-existent. If there were limits, there would be something outside God, another substance of the same nature, which is impossible (cf. *above*).

Let's move on to a whole series of propositions, some of which are obviously destined to take their place in a polemical discussion with "theologians" (these form the main category of "opponents" against whom the scolies are often directed). And let's come to a proposition that is crucial for what follows:

E1P29. In nature there is nothing contingent; but all things are determined by the necessity of divine nature to exist and produce an effect in a certain way.

This proposition expresses what we might call an absolute "necessitarianism". If there is no contingency, then all things obey determined causal mechanisms. As we can see, all conceptions of freedom as the power to choose indifferently, as free will, are incompatible with this proposition, unless they take man out of nature or make him "an empire within an empire".

The scolie (P29S) introduces a distinction taken from scholasticism, but once again completely diverted from its original purpose. Spinoza distinguishes:

- The "naturant" nature, i.e. God in himself, considered as the free cause and principle of existence of all that is.

- "Naturated" nature, i.e. everything that necessarily follows from God's nature, i.e. the differentiated reality of all things that exist in a determinate manner—i.e. obeying the laws of nature, which are nothing other than God's freedom (since freedom consists in acting according to the laws of one's own nature).

The following propositions (P30 and P31) set out what "understanding in act" is, which "must include the attributes and affections of God and nothing else." Understanding is not, then, a faculty that belongs to who knows what or who knows whom, a specific faculty whose use must be regulated. Understanding is actual (effective) and is summed up in the act of understanding. More precisely:

E1P31. Understanding in act, whether finite or infinite, as well as will, desire, love, etc., must be related to Nature Naturée, but not to Naturante.

Understanding is a "mode of thinking", as the demonstration makes clear, in the same way as will, love, etc., and is therefore an effect of the chain of causes and effects, with a "naturalized nature", in the same way as desire or love, even if it differs from them in essence. What this proposition means is what will be developed in Part II, and above all in Parts III and IV: to consider the human spirit as a mode, an affection of the eternal and infinite substance like the others. We must therefore draw all the consequences of this necessitarianism announced in P29. At the same time, we need to track down to their last refuges the prejudices concerning freedom as freedom of the will or pure contingency. Thus:

E1P32. The will cannot be called a free cause, but only a necessary cause.

Hence corollary I follows:

E1P32C1. It follows from this: 1° that God does not produce his effects through the freedom of his will.

And again:

E1P33. Things could not have been produced by God otherwise than they were or in another order.

And the scolie drives the point home:

E1P33S1. [...] there is absolutely nothing in things that allows us to call them contingent [...].

The scolie then gives definitions for necessary, impossible and contingent. NECESSARY is a thing because of its essence (for example, substance is necessary) or because of its cause (the cause exists, the effect necessarily exists). Necessary is opposed not by contingent but by IMPOSSIBLE: a thing is impossible if its essence contains a contradiction (e.g., a square circle), or if there is no external cause determined to produce it. What is necessary exists, and what does not exist is impossible. The CONTINGENT IS therefore that which appears to us (through a lack of knowledge) as neither necessary nor impossible. For example, a thing whose essence we don't know contains a contradiction appears to us as possible, even if it doesn't currently exist. A thing of which we are unaware that the causes that can produce it exist also appears to us as a possible thing, and we can even imagine that its existence depends solely on our free will. Conversely, a thing that currently exists, but for which we don't know what caused it, appears contingent. We believe that when we throw a die, it's chance that decides which number will come up, but if we knew the speed and direction of the throw, the physical properties of the die, the height from which it is thrown, and many other things besides, in law we should be able to predict exactly what the result of the throw will be. But since we can't in practice, we accept that "chance has decided". It seems that chance or contingency is just another way of talking about our ignorance. The question is obviously of the utmost importance when it comes to the natural sciences. Galilean and Newtonian physics are entirely deterministic, and regard randomness as nothing more than a (hopefully provisional) mark of our ignorance.

The Spinozist thesis could be related to a problem raised in the following century. If we know the present state of the world and the laws of nature, then the state of the world within a given period of time is predictable. This is Laplace's famous principle: "We must consider the present state of the universe as the effect of its previous state, and as the cause of that which will follow. An intelligence which, for a given instant, knew all the forces of which nature is animated and the respective situations of the beings which compose it, if moreover it were vast enough to submit these data to analysis, would embrace in the same formula the movements of the largest bodies in the universe and those of the lightest atom: nothing would be uncertain for it, and the future, like the past, would be present to its eyes[6]."

However, Laplace's formulation seems rather different from Spinoza's. Indeed, P29 does not imply Laplace's principle. Indeed, P29 does not imply Laplace's principle: we can perfectly well admit that there are deterministic theories without any capacity for prediction—this is the case, for example, in most of the historical sciences, such as the Darwinian theory of evolution. The Spinozist proposition can also be seen as an ontological thesis—it concerns the nature of what is, or, to use Spinoza's phrase, "the nature of things". Laplace's assertion, on the other hand, is gnoseological: it concerns what understanding can grasp about the nature of things. Moreover, Laplace's

---

6. Parmenides maintained that thinking and being are the same thing.

assertion must be properly understood: it concerns an infinite intelligence, not a human intelligence. For a human intelligence, it is impossible to grasp "all the forces of which nature is animated", which is why this reflection is placed at the beginning of a work dedicated to the calculation of probabilities: probabilities enable us to approach what would otherwise be forever beyond our reach. However, this gnoseological/ontological distinction is irrelevant to the metaphysics of *Ethics*.

This question was raised again at the beginning of the 20th century with the introduction of Heisenberg's "uncertainty principle". We have already had occasion to challenge the idea commonly held by philosophers (and some physicists) that quantum physics, which is fundamentally statistical physics, calls into question the principle of determinism (see our *La matière et l'esprit*, Armand Colin, 2004). But the debate is not over. It would seem, however, that even if there are no "hidden variables" in contemporary physics, Spinozist necessitarianism is at least a far more productive hypothesis than that of admitting that there is randomness in nature.

The following scolie (P33S2) clarifies a number of decisive questions, which also need to be explained.

E1P33S2. From the foregoing it clearly follows that things were produced by God according to a supreme perfection, since they necessarily followed from a sovereignly perfect nature. And this does not impute any imperfection to God, for it is his very perfection that has compelled us to affirm it.

Chapter I: "On God" or the Nature of Things Demonstrated *ordine geometrico*

From the perfection of God, we must deduce the perfection of what is! If there were a Creator God, it's almost natural to think that there's less in the creature than in the Creator. But since there is no Creator God, the problem is posed in a completely different way. A thing that exists, exists because of determined causes, and therefore it exists exactly as it "had" to exist, since "things could not have been produced by God otherwise than they were, nor in any other order" (P33). So if it is exactly as it should be, it is perfect, imperfection being merely the mark of incompleteness or non-conformity between plan and realization. Those who don't want to understand this judge things by their imagination, not by their understanding.

Spinoza accuses those who reject this thesis of attributing imperfection to God. If, in fact, God produces imperfect things, and if he could have done otherwise than produce them as they are, then he is imperfect, and therefore not God.

Once again, the disagreement stems from the consideration of freedom. Those who reject the Spinozist position attribute to God an absolute will, which is a "futility" and "a great obstacle to science". Nevertheless, to convince the doubters, Spinoza adds a new demonstration by admitting that God has a will. In this case, too, things can only be as they are, otherwise we could still attribute imperfection to God. Finally, and this is the decisive argument, if everything exists by divine decree, this decree is from all eternity. Now, "in eternity, there is neither *when*, nor *before*, nor *after*" (E1P33S2), and so God is not before his decrees, nor after his decrees, so things can only be one way. Here we see the importance of eternity. God is eternal, which is precisely the same as refuting the idea of creation, since creation presupposes a God prior to it, a transcendent God. In Spinozian metaphysics, immanence and eternity are absolutely interchangeable.

We won't go any further in analyzing this demonstration, which repeats arguments that have already been made. The end, however, is noteworthy:

E1P33S2. [...] I recognize, moreover, that this opinion, which subjects all things to God's indifferent will and admits that they all depend on his good pleasure, is less far from the truth than the opinion of those who admit that God acts in all things with a view to good.

This "opinion" is an aspect of Cartesian doctrine that Spinoza does not share, but which, on balance, is better than the belief that God acts for good, which Spinoza characterizes here as an "absurdity". This absurdity will be further demolished in the appendix to Part I.

E1P34. God's power is his very essence.

It's absolutely obvious, like the following:

E1P35. All that we conceive to be in the power of God, is necessarily.

Chapter I: "On God" or the Nature of Things Demonstrated *ordine geometrico*

Again what we conceive and what is correspond. If we conceive something to be in God's power, it must be. Abysmal truth! The question now is how we can adequately conceive of what is in God's power. This will be one of the issues of Part Two.

Finalism and Superstition: Appendix to Part I

The appendix to Part I is a short treatise on superstition and the formation of traditional religions. How we move from the prejudices to which men are naturally inclined to the formation of delusional ideas is the subject of the appendix.

The appendix concludes Part I ("**By the foregoing I have explained the nature of God and his properties...**"), and this first moment of the appendix sums up the achievements of the first part.

- God necessarily exists (God is the eternal, infinite substance with infinite attributes).

- All things are in God and depend on him (nothing can be or be conceived outside God, Spinoza repeats).

- There is no arbitrary "will of God", God has no whims: everything that is proceeds from God, is "predetermined" by God according to his absolute nature. "Predetermined" must be understood correctly. It does not mean that things proceed from a finalized will. "Predetermined" must be understood not as "premeditated", but as arising from determined causes.

The stone falls because it is predetermined to fall, not because God "willed" the stone to fall, but because the laws of nature are such that the stone falls and nothing else. "God's infinite power" is nothing other than the laws of nature, which are also the laws of divine nature.

Part I examined a number of prejudices that prevent us from understanding the demonstrations of the *Ethics*. Suffice it here to recall the scolie of proposition XV ("There are some who imagine God composed all like a man"), which attacks anthropomorphism, i.e. this conception of God as the projection of an image of man. This proposition continues in proposition E1P16, whose scolie develops what is meant by God's power, refusing to attribute to God a will and an understanding in the very sense in which we use these terms when we apply them to humans.

The aim of this appendix is to continue the examination of the prejudices that were left out of the first part. The precise purpose of the appendix is to submit to the scrutiny of reason those prejudices which "prevent men from grasping the sequence of things". What, then, is the main prejudice that prevents men from correctly grasping the real sequence of things? It's the "finalist" prejudice, the one that precisely inverts the order of cause and effect, and claims that the effect is the true cause: "Men commonly suppose that all natural things act as they do, in view of an end, and much more they consider it certain that God disposes of everything in view of a certain end."

We can already point out something: it's not just a question of denouncing prejudices as irrational, but above all of understanding the reasons for them, i.e. the mechanisms by which prejudices are produced (which, like all things, are "predetermined") and also what prejudices produce, which, like all ideas, are also the causes of other ideas.

This first introductory moment of the appendix closes with the exposition of a plan that we recall here:

1) Why do men like this prejudice?

2) Demonstrating the falsity of prejudice?

3) Examination of its consequences as the matrix of all superstitious beliefs.

Why do men indulge in finalistic prejudice? Origin and nature of finalist prejudice

Let's begin by summarizing Spinoza's essential thesis here: all prejudices have a common core, which is the belief in "final causes"; if man falls into the prejudice of attributing final causes to nature, this is a consequence of the fact that he is a being of desire, and therefore of his nature, and consequently this prejudice is by no means irrational in the sense that it is "predetermined" as soon as we truly know human nature. Belief in final causes is thus a kind of rationalization of what guides man in the fulfillment of his desires.

The argumentation is strictly demonstrative. Each assured truth must produce all its effects, since "there is no thing whose nature does not give rise to some effect" (E1P36).

From each truth are deduced the propositions that follow by logical inference. Let's summarize this argument in a few propositions.

(1) Men are born without knowledge of causes, but only with an awareness of their appetites.

(2) Ignorance of causes makes them believe they are free.

(3) Men always act with an end in view.

(4) They therefore tend to assume final causes everywhere.

(5) This tendency is reinforced by the fact that they know themselves better than they know other beings, and therefore project their own complexion onto other beings.

Let's take a closer look at the sequence of these theses.

The first three lines set out the proposition that men are born without knowledge of the causes of things, but only with an appetite for what is useful to them. Let's begin by noting that appetite is the appetite for what is useful. All being tends to persevere in its being," Spinoza often says. So appetite is not something that should be condemned or controlled, as a tradition that unites some of the Greek philosophers and most Christians demands. For a Platonist or a Christian, appetite is not only bad because it relates to sensible things, but also wrong; it has the wrong goal and leads us into suffering. For Spinoza, there's no such thing. What's more, this appetite for what is useful to them is not something purely corporeal, since they are conscious of it; indeed, it is insofar as it is conscious of itself that appetite is called Desire (cf. *below*). The appetite for what is useful, and the consciousness that

77

accompanies it, are therefore not accidents or bad tendencies that can be rid of through meditation, asceticism or catharsis. On the contrary, they are part and parcel of man's essence. It is impossible to think of Spinozist man without first thinking of this fundamental tendency, this "effort", this *conatus* that is both irresistible impulse and conscious aim[7]. But this conscious appetite exists in a man who is unaware of the real causes of things, and particularly of the causes that make him exist, that make him have such and such a desire or such and such an appetite. A number of important consequences follow from this, which are outside the precise scope of our study, but should be noted immediately: for example, the will is not a human faculty as such, since men are determined to want this or that thing that is useful to them.

It is this combination of ignorance of real causes and awareness of the ends of what moves us that is, according to Spinoza, the explanation for man's most common prejudices. The first of these prejudices is that of our own freedom. Spinoza tells us that "men believe themselves to be free, because they are conscious of their volitions and appetites, and do not think, even in dreams, of the causes which dispose them to desire and will, because they are ignorant of them". This sentence is a direct polemic against Descartes. Descartes, in fact, considers freedom to be a self-evident fact

---

7. Kant would return to this distinction between extensive and intensive quantities.

of consciousness. In the *Principles of Philosophy*, Descartes states that "The principal perfection of man is to have free will". What does free will mean? In his *Letter to Father Mesland* (February 9, 1645), Descartes clarifies: "It is always possible to turn us away from pursuing a clearly known good, or from admitting an obvious truth, provided only that we consider it a good thus to attest the freedom of our free will." On what is this evidence based? On the inner experience that I have the possibility of affirming or denying, according to my will, says Descartes: "I cannot also complain that God has not given me a free will, or a will sufficiently ample and perfect; since indeed I experience it so vague and extensive that it is not enclosed within any boundaries[8]." Descartes thus bases freedom on our awareness of our volitions. But here Spinoza overturns Cartesianism. Volition is not free, and if we consider it to be so, it is only out of ignorance, since, "even in dreams", men do not think "of the causes that dispose them to desire and will". Desiring and willing are in fact one and the same act, and the will, conceived in its autonomy, appears to be an illusion of the imagination, which ruins the conception of freedom as free will that underpins Cartesian philosophy. As a corollary, the thesis of the will as a faculty of the soul, and more generally the Cartesian theory of the faculties of the soul in general, is also ruined.

---

8. Laplace (Pierre-Simon, de), *Essai philosophique sur les probabilités* (1814), electronic edition on the Bibliothèque Vigdor website, p. 3, (www.vigdor. com/titres/laplaceEssaiPhilosophiqueProba.html).

Chapter I: "On God" or the Nature of Things Demonstrated *ordine geometrico*

What characterizes human appetite and volition is that they are always directed towards a goal, a particular end. The action resulting from volition is therefore always an action carried out with a view to something useful. The principle of utility is a consequence of the definition of being as effort, appetite or desire. Being aims at what seems useful to persevere in its being. In the sections on the affections of the soul and the servitude of man, Spinoza sets out all the ethical consequences of this principle of utility; in particular, he describes the Good as that which is truly useful, and Evil as that which harms us. Here, the principle of utility desi-gnates the precise direction of effort, and what kinds of ends are targeted.

The preceding propositions allow us to infer this fourth thesis concerning belief in final causes. The chain of reasoning can be summarized as follows:

(1) Man is unaware of the true causes.

(2) Consciously acting for a purpose that is useful to him.

(3) So the only causality he is spontaneously led to believe in is the one he experiences himself, i.e. the final cause.

Spinoza was not the first to denounce the use of final causes as contrary to the true exercise of reason. The Cartesians, Descartes and Malebranche, were categorical on this point. But Spinoza was the first to go right to the root of finalist belief, showing the mechanism by which illusion is generated in human nature itself. Let's be clear: this is not a question of questioning man's finitude, weakness or corruption, themes found in most philosophers who contemplate man's nature. For Spinoza, prejudice and delusion are not manifestations of human imperfection to be criticized, condemned, deplored or denounced, but results of the necessary movement in which nature occurs. Man, Spinoza tells us, is not an "empire within an empire"; he is therefore subject to necessary laws that determine him to do this or that thing as a consequence of what he is by nature.

The last part of the reasoning aims to explain how men are led to extrapolate to the whole of nature what they are aware of about their own actions, since, on the one hand, they "necessarily judge of the complexion of others by their own", and, on the other, they interpret everything they find in nature that is useful to them as being made on purpose for them, "as means for their own utility". First of all, then, it is the mode of reasoning by superficial analogy, whose impotence is shown here, that leads to error; this mode of reasoning corresponds to what Spinoza calls in the *Treatise on the Reform of the Understanding*, knowledge of the second kind[9], defined as follows: "There is a perception acquired by vague experience, that is, by an experience which is not determined by the understanding; so called only because, having fortuitously offered itself and having been contradicted by no other, it has remained as if unshaken within us." It is this

---

9. The role of appetite is emphasized in Aristotle's treatise *On the Soul*. Aristotle notes that the object of appetite is the starting point of executive intelligence.

Chapter I: "On God" or the Nature of Things Demonstrated ordine geometrico

inner experience, which Cartesians make the starting point of all true philosophy, that is here refuted as knowledge by "vague experience".

Let's understand what's at stake here: the finalist is the one who considers that things are ordered according to the order in which he imagines them. A thirsty man imagines that drinking a tall glass of fresh water will give him the greatest pleasure, and immediately heads for the fridge. He therefore believes that the cause of his movement towards the refrigerator is the purpose of the movement (to drink fresh water) and therefore he believes that the cause of his movement is an event that will happen afterwards (i.e. when he opens the refrigerator door). But to reason in this way is to reason according to the imagination, not according to the natural sequence of cause and effect. The real sequence is as follows: the man is thirsty, and thirst triggers an association of ideas (see E2P18). The image of the well-being provided by the glass of fresh water forms in his mind and triggers the movement towards the fridge. There is no "final cause" here. The cause of the movement is not the fact of drinking a glass of water (a later event), but the image formed in the mind, which is an earlier event and triggers the movement. Finalism thus turns everything on its head, inverting the real order into an imaginary one.

From prejudice to religious superstition

Spinoza then exposes the absurd consequences of this mode of reasoning, which consists in considering the whole of creation as destined for human use. The accumulation of finalist expressions—"eyes to see, teeth to chew"—is intended for rhetorical effect. We are dealing with a world of pure fantasy, where everything has been arranged for man! Nature seems animated, things seem endowed with intentions towards us.

From this stems another belief: since this arrangement looks miraculous, we assume a miracle-worker, a "someone else who has arranged these means to their use".

What follows is a veritable genealogy of religious superstition. Men invent beings of whom they obviously know nothing, and on whom they project what they know of themselves. So these "rectors" of nature must act as men, with human ends in view, and by means of human freedom. Men act in view of their own usefulness. If the gods arrange nature for man's convenience, it must be because they expect something in return, that men honor and worship them. The decisive passage is as follows: "From which it resulted that each of them, according to his own naturalness, invented various ways of worshipping God, so that God would love him more than all the others, and put the whole of nature at the service of his blind desire and insatiable greed. And so this prejudice became a superstition and sank deep roots in people's minds."

Chapter I: "On God" or the Nature of Things Demonstrated *ordine geometrico*

Note that the driving force behind prejudice and its transformation into superstition lies in desire and the imaginary fixations of desire. This entire passage thus sets out the (rationally comprehensible) causes of the birth of historical religions, which Spinoza equates purely and simply with superstitions. And these superstitions he also calls "delusions". Those who want to show that "Nature does nothing in vain" "seem only to have shown that Nature and the Gods are delirious as well as men." The expression "Nature does nothing in vain" recurs like a leitmotif in the writings of Aristotle, for whom reason is the end, and here Spinoza clearly assumes the rationalists' polemic against Aristotelian philosophy. The comparison of religious superstition to delirium was a frequent theme among Enlightenment thinkers. It was also used by Freud, who defined religious belief as a "delusional idea" in *The Future of an Illusion* (1927).

Why is it a delusion? Simply because superstition denies reality. Obviously, in nature many things go against human interests (diseases, storms, natural disasters, etc.), and what's more, these things strike pious and wicked men alike. This simple fact should be enough to challenge the prejudice that everything is ordered for the good of mankind. But "they therefore took it for granted that the judgments of the Gods are far beyond the reach of human intelligence". One of the Church Fathers, Tertullian, is credited with the phrase "I believe because it is absurd" (*Credo quia absurdum*)! Without going to that extreme, this is belief without rational proof, and even in defiance of rational proof.

Mathematics points the way to truth

The end of the paragraph is devoted to pointing the way out. Indeed, if men are naturally inclined to hold prejudices as true and are thus led into superstition, it might seem that the path to truth is obstructed, and one would even wonder how philosophers, being men, are able to recognize prejudice and delusion in common opinion.

Mathematics is the science that allows us to get away from habitual prejudices, because it deals only with the essences and properties of figures, and not with final causes. It also provides "rules of truth". These two parts are easy to understand.

1) Mathematics doesn't care about ends! A triangle is a triangle, and we know everything about it when we know its essence: its definition, which is at the same time its method of construction.

2) Mathematical truths proceed from demonstrations that produce certainty.

Of course, Spinoza is not saying that all truths are mathematical—he's careful not to make such bold and perilous claims as Galileo's that "the great book of nature is written in mathematical language". Spinoza confines himself to saying that mathematics is a model for those seeking truth. Like mathematicians, we have to deal with the nature of things (and not their alleged finality) and proceed by demonstrations (*more geometrico*).

Chapter I: "On God" or the Nature of Things Demonstrated *ordine geometrico*

Finalism is false

Here, Spinoza builds on what was shown earlier.

- E1P16: *From the necessity of the divine nature must follow an infinity of things in an infinity of modes (i.e. everything that can fall under an infinite understanding).* This proposition affirms the infinite productivity of God (or Nature). He who seeks final causes does so because the infinity of things that proceed from the divine nature escapes him. He would need an "infinite understanding". But his understanding is only finite... By reducing the infinite to the finite, he is condemned to a truncated grasp of the sequence of things, and thus gives free rein to his imagination.

- E1P32 (corollaries): These corollaries establish that *God does not produce his effects through the freedom of his will* (C1) and that there is no such thing as a free will, because the will must in turn be determined (C2).

The appendix merely completes and illustrates these fundamental propositions.

Finalist doctrine "turns Nature upside down". As we've already emphasized, it inverts the real order by interchanging causes and effects: the effect is taken to be the cause, under the name of "final cause". But it also inverts the more perfect and the less perfect. This whole passage is a little complex, and deserves a closer look.

The propositions XXI, XXII and XXIII to which Spinoza refers concern the way in which God produces his effects. Proposition XXI asserts that what follows absolutely from an attribute of God must always have existed, and is infinite. If you think about it, this is almost absolutely obvious. If B proceeds from A, and A is eternal, then B eternally proceeds from A. The same reasoning applies if A is infinite. So everything that follows from an attribute of God is eternal and infinite. Everything that follows from a modified attribute, likewise every mode that necessarily exists and is infinite, proceeds either from the "absolute" nature of an attribute of God or from a modified attribute. In short, everything that proceeds immediately from God (i.e., without mediation) is infinite. God alone is a "free cause", and all things that are exist only as an affirmation of God's power to exist. Finite things, those that do not exist immediately but as the effect of something else, express a lesser power to exist, and are therefore less perfect. Finalism, on the other hand, makes God's perfection a consequence of the existence of finite things (for example, men created for the greater glory of God.) So finalism makes what is perfect depend on what is less perfect! Another inversion of reality.

This finalist doctrine therefore contradicts the idea of divine perfection. If God acts with a view to his own perfection (for example, by creating mankind), then he is lacking something and is not perfect—a manifest absurdity, according to Spinoza, since there can be nothing more perfect than God, i.e. "a substance constituted by an infinity of attributes, each of which expresses an eternal and infinite essence" (E1P11).

Chapter I: "On God" or the Nature of Things Demonstrated ordine geometrico

***The chain of cause and effect is sufficient to explain all
natural things.***

The preceding critique of finalism may seem like a refutation by the absurd: to admit finalism is to deny the propositions demonstrated in the preceding pages. The point is to show that finalism is useless, since what it claims to explain can be explained in another way, by making much less costly assumptions. To avoid scientific understanding, in the natural order (from the anterior to the posterior, from causes to effects), finalist explanation invents hypotheses devoid of any foundation, all of which boil down to a mysterious will of God, which Spinoza says is "the asylum of ignorance."

Let's take a look at one of the examples used:

> *In the same way, faced with the structure of the human body, they are astonished and, ignoring the causes of so much art, they conclude that this structure is not due to a mechanical art but to a divine or supernatural art, and that it is formed in such a way that no part harms the other.*

Indeed, it is the attempt to understand living things that most often lends an air of sanity to finalist prejudices. The complexity of living things far exceeds our ability to grasp the physico-chemical sequences of complex systems, and the temptation is great to imagine, in these extraordinary arrangements that are living things, a finality ordered by some "great architect". Thus, Jean-Baptiste Lamarck, one of the first scientists to conceive of the evolutionary kinship of all living beings, believed that there was a kind of drive towards complexification as living beings sought to adapt to their environment. Darwin, on the other hand, sought to stick to mechanisms of pure causality, without involving either general evolutionary tendencies or final causes: only random modifications of certain characters allow us to understand the evolution of living beings, when these characters appear without a determined plan and prove to be favorable or unfavorable to the survival of the individual. Defenders of Lamarckian evolution, however, insist on the need for "intelligent design": an organ as complex as the eye, they claim, cannot result from a random selective process, as Darwinians maintain.

If, in nature, every event happens by virtue of determined causes, we must reject belief in miracles, and if something seems extraordinary, we must strive to find "the true causes" and "understand natural things as a scientist instead of being astonished by them like a fool".

Spinoza ends this development by pointing out the responsibility of "those whom the vulgar adores as the true interpreters of Nature and the Gods". Theologians, gurus, false scientists, impostors and charlatans of all kinds—these hold their authority only from the ignorance of the "vulgar". If, on the contrary, the scientist sheds light on the real process and dispels belief in miracles, they prosecute him as impious. We can assume that Spinoza is thinking here of the

Chapter I: "On God" or the Nature of Things Demonstrated ordine geometrico

persecution Galileo had to endure for arguing the motion of the Earth and the common physical nature of the Earth and "heavens". The question of superstition therefore has a political dimension: rational knowledge of nature and the destruction of prejudice undermine false authorities. The link between the progress of knowledge and political emancipation was to be one of the main themes of the Enlightenment, and this link was already clearly established by Spinoza, who appears in every respect to be the first great philosopher of the Enlightenment.

Consequences concerning Good, Evil, Beautiful, Ugly, etc.

As we've seen, finalist prejudice consists in reducing everything to the self. Nature is ordered in relation to us: "Noses were made to wear glasses, so we have glasses", says Voltaire to his Pangloss; or again, according to Bernardin de Saint-Pierre (*Harmonies naturelles*), "The melon was divided into slices by nature to be eaten as a family; the pumpkin, being larger, can be eaten with the neighbors." Bringing everything back to himself, the finalist projects onto the outside world what he knows of himself, judges everything in relation to himself, and transforms into a determination of the essence of things what belongs solely to the subjective relationship he has with them.

Spinoza concludes the appendix with a genealogy of shared values, which he shows to have no objective character but depend entirely on our imagination.

Relativity of Good and Evil

Therefore, whatever contributes to the health and worship of God, men have called Good; whatever is contrary to them, they have called Evil. And since those who do not understand the nature of things are incapable of asserting anything about them, but only imagine them and take imagination for understanding, they therefore believe that there is order in things, ignorant as they are both of the nature of things and of their own.

The Good, then, has no objective determination: men call it what they judge to be favourable to them, and again according to what they imagine, since most of the time they "mistake imagination for understanding". Likewise, when they speak of the natural order, they are content to imagine according to their desires. But objectively, i.e. "in God", there is neither good nor evil. The extinction of the great saurians was an evil for the dinosaurs, and a finalist dinosaur would have sought some reason for this misfortune, in which men would have been quick to see proof of Providence, which is doubtless not the opinion of the species extinguished from the planet by human action.

Extending the approach to other concepts

The same applies, of course, to other notions, such as Beauty and Ugliness, and so on. But beauty does not reside

Chapter I: "On God" or the Nature of Things Demonstrated *ordine geometrico*

in nature, but only in the imagination: "harmony has made men lose their reason; did they not believe that God too was delighted by it? There were even philosophers who believed that celestial movements compose a harmony. In this highly polemical development, Platonic idealism and Augustinianism are once again targeted.

"As many heads, as many opinions".

As all these notions of Good and Evil, Beautiful and Ugly, are subjective, it is natural that men judge each according to his own naturalness. One will find ugly what another finds beautiful. In a very materialistic way, Spinoza even says that everyone judges "according to the disposition of their brain", not according to their understanding! Indeed, mathematics shows that everyone agrees when faced with demonstrations, so when men use their understanding, they can all be of the same opinion.

Here we see the outline of a theme that will recur in the third and fourth parts: as long as they are subject to their affections—that is, to knowledge through the imagination— men are often hostile to one another, whereas they agree with one another when they are guided by right reason.

In conclusion, all these notions are simply ways of imagining, not objective knowledge. If we understand this, we can also see that there is no imperfection in nature in the vulgar sense of the word. There are only degrees of power that derive from the implementation of natural laws. Animals that only

92

follow their animal instincts are at a lower level of power than man, who can also follow his reason. But to follow his reason, he must begin to rid himself, as far as he is able, of the phantasmagoria of superstition.

Chapter II:
"The Nature of the Human Mind", or Mental Reality

To understand Part II, we must always bear in mind the definition of God given in Part I, which Spinoza recalls in the preamble to Part II: "**God, in other words, the eternal and infinite Being**".

We perceive two attributes of God: thought and extent. We can therefore know God under two attributes, either as extent (nature) or as a "thinking thing".

The Reality of Ideas

Let's also remember that everything that is, is in God. So all bodies are part of nature... and all ideas (thoughts) are part of reality as a thinking thing. The singular ideas or thoughts we have in mind right now, for example, are finite modes of God considered as a thinking thing. All this may seem a little strange to us, who tend to regard ideas only as subjective mental states, somehow devoid of any objective reality. But a clear understanding of what "eternal and infinite Being" is will help us to grasp it better. Everyone can easily accept the idea of an eternal and infinite nature. This eternal and infinite nature constantly produces, by its own laws, all kinds of finite beings ("finite modes of the infinite substance") which are affected in a thousand and one ways by other finite beings. Each of these finite modes perceived under the attribute of extent corresponds to an idea. For example, we don't know whether there are living extraterrestrial beings, but if there are, there are also ideas whose object (ideat) is these extraterrestrials. Ideas themselves, independently of the reality of their object (e.g. fictions), are themselves realities, for each of which there exists an idea, the idea of the idea. So thought is one order of reality, just as expanse is another (though we can't establish a hierarchy between the two).

We can therefore conceive of a being "from which must follow an infinity of things in an infinity of modes (i.e. everything that can fall under an infinite understanding)" (E1P16). In God, then, "is necessarily the idea both of his essence and of all that necessarily follows from his essence" (E2P3). Of course, we ourselves, with our finite understanding, can't grasp all that! But just because we can't grasp the infinite number of things in detail, one by one, doesn't mean they don't exist. One of the causes of error is precisely that we tend (by nature) to reduce everything to our finite understanding—that is, to take a (small) part for the whole.

The Formal Nature of Ideas and Truth: The Double Aspect of Ideas and the Critique of the Theory of Representation

Proposition V introduces the notion of the **formal being of ideas**. An idea can be considered in two ways: as such, i.e. as an idea that has God as its cause; and in its relation to its object. Let's put it another way, using an example: the idea of Paul that I currently have in my mind is a "mental state" (to use the modern language of the philosophy of mind).

-This mental state is produced as the effect of other mental states: an old image of Paul, associated with that novel we'd been passionately discussing, and an allusion to that novel in an article I'm reading right now that brings the idea of Paul back to my mind. The order and connection of these mental states, which are "the same as the order and connection of things" (E2P7), are well inserted into the set of causal relations by which everything that exists is produced.

-This mental state (the current idea of Paul in my mind) has an object (or ideat) which is my friend Paul, but this mental state does not "represent" Paul. It is an image of him.

It is therefore possible to separate the idea itself from what it is supposed to represent—to separate the intrinsic

97

properties of the idea from its extrinsic properties. This way of thinking about ideas (i.e., mental reality) radically excludes all conceptions that reduce mental states to mere representations of physical states, or even to mere epiphenomena. This is where Spinoza's materialist interpretations can no longer work. For a classical materialist, the only reality is physical (extended), and the mind is merely an illusion or epiphenomenon of physical reality. The only problem for this kind of materialism is to understand how physical reality produces mental reality, so the essential link is between the idea and what it represents. Nothing of the sort for Spinoza. The link between the idea and what it represents is an extrinsic one (which, as we shall see, is always equivocal). Ideas are real, but their object may not be, as in the case of fictions, or may represent only a truncated perception of reality. Ideas are "adequate" insofar as they are considered "without relation to an object" and have "all the intrinsic properties [ ] of a true idea" (E2D4). The "true idea" is therefore not the copy of a reality, as in the classical definition of truth (adequacy of thought to the thing), since the idea is also a reality, but of another order. In a letter to Tschirnhaus, Spinoza clarifies his thinking: "I recognize no difference between the true idea and the adequate idea, except that the word true refers to the agreement of the idea with its object, whereas the word adequate refers to the nature of the idea in itself. There is therefore no difference between a true idea and an adequate idea apart from this extrinsic relation."

Spontaneous and Reflexive Knowledge

Propositions XIV to XIX set out the mechanisms of spontaneous knowledge. E2P16 links the ideas formed by the mind with the affections of the body. The only ideas we have are those of bodily modifications. Corollary II emphasizes that "the ideas we have of external bodies indicate rather the constitution of our own body than the nature of external bodies" (E2P16C2). Put another way: when we perceive a certain thing, the idea we have is not the idea of the thing itself, but only the idea of the effect of the thing on us, and we take this effect of the thing on us to be the thing itself. This is a source of confusion, which led Spinoza to say that knowledge through the senses is confused (it always mixes the idea of the thing with the affection that the thing produces on our body).

The power of imagination

E2P17 explains the origin of judgments of existence. In it, we learn that the existence of things is not self-evident, is not something that is given, but a judgment not of the thing itself but of the mind's affections. In other words, judgments of existence are indeed imaginary, even though they are part of the normal functioning of the soul. In effect, this proposition establishes that our body keeps track of the modifications it has undergone from the outside, as long as nothing erases them. At the same time, we understand (as a

99

corollary of E2P17) how we can imagine as present a body that is not present.

The scolie clarifies what Spinoza means by imagination: imagination is the action of the mind forming images of the bodies it posits as present; and these images are the ideas of bodily affections. This scolie deserves to be explained in some detail. We start from E2P13, which asserted that the human body exists as we feel it. (Spinoza does not for a minute discuss the idea that we might not have a body, or any of the other "extravagant suppositions of the skeptics" as Descartes puts them in the First Meditation).

A distinction must be made between the following:

1° The idea of Peter (which is the essence of Peter's spirit) which has as its object the essence of Peter's body and expresses it for as long as the body currently exists.

2° Paul's idea of Peter, which expresses the state of Paul's body and lasts as long as Paul's body lasts (for example, when Paul looks at Peter, there is a certain idea of Peter in his mind that lasts as long as Paul looks at Peter from the same angle).

Hence the definition of *images*: affections of the human body whose ideas represent external things to us as being present, even if they do not reproduce the figures of things. Note here the distinction between image and figure: an image is simply the idea of the affection of my body produced by an external body. It is neither a diagram nor a kind of detached part of the thing that has come into my mind. It may have nothing to do with the essence of the thing. The figure, on the other hand, indicates something of the essence of the thing (the figure of the circle says something of the essence of the circle as that which is generated by the rotation of a segment around one of its extremities). The contemplation of bodies in images is *imagination.*

Imagination is not error," says Spinoza. It is error only insofar as we do not know at the same time that the thing imagined is not actually present, or does not have the figure that imagination gives us. Imagining a winged horse is not an error. It is an error only when, at the same time, the idea that winged horses do not exist is not present in the mind. We could translate this distinction as the distinction between imagination and illusion. In *The Future of Illusion,* Freud makes a clear distinction between imagination as a normal function of the psyche and delusions.

The last part of the scolie is unclear. If the mind knew, at the same time as it imagines a thing, that this thing does not currently exist, it would attribute this power to a virtue and see it as a manifestation of its freedom. However, Spinoza expresses all this in the conditional tense, and so it seems that more often than not, unable as we are to clearly understand all these spontaneous mechanisms of knowledge, we are incapable, by the same token, of wisely using our imagination as a virtue or a power. Ignorant men allow themselves to be guided by their imagination and become delirious (see appendix to E1, or the preface to the *Traité théologico-politique*).

E2P18 explains memory through image association. It is thus explained that the linking of words can be done without recourse to images. If the image of A has often been associated with the image of B, the word A will immediately evoke the word B. So we can repeat sentences without really knowing anything. Knowledge that is merely the knowledge of words (hearsay, as Spinoza put it) is fundamentally equivocal. We need to distinguish between signs (words and other signs produced by the imagination) and concepts. The sign "circle" is a kind of image that evokes the idea of a circle. But if I use the word "circle" to refer to a hoop played with by a child, or a crudely drawn picture in the sand, it's clear that the sign and the essence of the circle don't correspond.

To summarize these proposals XVI to XVIII, we would like to highlight the following points:

-Perception is a psycho-physiological mechanism: it is the affection of my body by another body that is expressed in perception.

-Judgment is not involved in perception.

-Imagination is defined as the persistence of a perception in the body.

-We have a physiological theory of memory retention.

So there is no special power of the mind, no recourse to interiority as a source of faculties. It's a surprising paradox: Spinozist psychology is not that of a rationalist, but closely resembles that of an empiricist. In many respects, these last propositions are very similar to those of Hobbes (see the first chapters of *Leviathan*), even in their sequence. Everything asserted there, says Spinoza, is "solidly established by experience." Many commentators on Spinoza fail to emphasize this central role of experience.

Mind and body again. The genesis of consciousness

Proposition XIX asserts that the mind knows the body only through ideas of the affections it is affected by (I know my lungs because smoke makes me cough!).

It's important to emphasize once again: "the mind *is* the idea of the body", not "the mind *has* the idea of the body". This is a far-reaching proposition. In the reality that I am, perceived as an expanse or as an idea (mind), there is no "I" who possesses it all, the body, the ideas. What the speaker calls "I" is that reality in which there is thought. If we take a great leap forward in the history of philosophy, we'll find Nietzsche mocking this "good old I" as a pure grammatical illusion, and it's possible to draw many threads between Spinoza and Nietzsche. In a philosophy of immanence such as Spinoza's, there is no room for a transcendental "I" as we find in Kant. There are processes and the ideas of these processes, but no subject. A "process without a subject".

The following propositions (XX to XXIII) deal with the genesis of consciousness, a genesis that indeed proceeds from the spontaneous functioning of the mind. Let's begin with Proposition XX. "Of the human mind there is also in God the idea or knowledge", meaning that there is a reality of the

Chapter II: "The Nature of the Human Mind", or Mental Reality

human mind independent of the knowledge we have of it. There is an idea of the body (the spirit) and an idea of this idea. This idea of the mind is explicitly related by Spinoza to the mind as an idea of the body. In other words, as the body is given, there is at the same time the idea of the body and the idea of this idea, as stated in proposition XXI. This can be understood more clearly, says Spinoza (E2P21S), by the scolie of proposition VII, to which we must return.

Spinoza reminds us that certain Hebrews seem to have perceived "as if in a fog" an essential truth: "God, God's understanding and the things understood by him are one and the same thing". God is not a person with faculties (understanding) that produce ideas. God is nothing other than these ideas in act, which constitute the divine understanding and God himself. What's difficult to understand is simply that we need to break with the idea of a transcendent God, a God who is a person or power outside reality. Instead, we need to place ourselves on a plane of radical immanence. Creator and creation are the same thing, and the terms creator and creation become completely inappropriate. Spinoza gives an example to illustrate what some Hebrews saw "as in a mist". The circle that exists in Nature and the idea of the circle that is also in God (*Deus sive natura!* "God, that is, nature!") are the same thing, whose essence is perceived under two different attributes. Therefore, whichever attribute we perceive nature under, we find "one and the same order", "one and the same connection of causes". But Spinoza goes on to show why a clear distinction must be drawn between thought and extent. "And when I said that God is the cause of the idea, for example of the circle only in so far as it is a thinking thing, and of the circle only in so far as it is an extended thing, it is only because the formal being of the idea of the circle can only be perceived by another mode of thinking which is like its next cause, this in turn by another and so on ad infinitum;": a body can only act on a body and only an idea (a mode of thinking) can perceive another idea. I perceive the idea of a circle by means of the idea of a point, a segment, a rotation, and the circle is generated by the rotation of a segment. But the idea of rotation of a segment doesn't generate a circle, but the idea of a circle. Or the idea of a dog will surely produce the idea of barking, but the idea of a dog does not bark. So Spinoza, while saying that the circle and the idea of a circle are the same thing, could be maintaining a kind of dualism that is perhaps not as far removed from Cartesian dualism as one might think. There is a monism of substance, but a dualism of attributes, of what "the understanding perceives of substance as constituting its essence" (E1D4). Conclusion: "Insofar as we regard things as modes of thinking, we must explain the order of the whole of Nature, in other words the connection of causes, by the sole attribute of Thought."

Let us now return to Proposition XXI. The idea of mind and mind are one and the same thing. But unlike the circle example, it's one and the same thing "conceived under one and the same attribute". Why does this "one and the same thing" split into two? Because the idea of spirit is like the form of spirit. The mind is the idea of the body. It is therefore considered in relation to the body, which constitutes its ideate. The idea of mind considers mind in itself, "without relation to an object". The idea of spirit says that spirit *is*. What the mind *is*, we'll see in the relationship between mind and body. He who knows something knows at the same time that he knows that he knows, and so on ad infinitum.

The following two propositions show that the mind knows not only the affections of the Body, but also the ideas of these affections, and that the mind knows itself only insofar as it perceives the ideas of the affections of the Body. This means that the spontaneous knowledge we have of our own mind is always subject to the regime of the knowledge we have of our body, i.e. a truncated and more often than not confused knowledge. The conclusions are developed in propositions XXIV to XXXI: the spontaneous ideas we form of things, by perceiving them through imaginary representations, are all inadequate, starting with the ideas we form of our own body (which, as we shall see, we don't know what it can do!) and the ideas we form of our own mind.

These propositions show that knowledge by imagination ("knowledge of the first kind") does not lead to adequate ideas. It is from proposition XXXII onwards that the possibility of the mind having adequate knowledge is set out.

Why Error is Always Only Relative

Proposition XXXII is surprising at first glance.

E2P32. All ideas, insofar as they are related to God, are true.

They are true "in relation to God", i.e. grasped in the sequence by which they are produced, because they agree with their object, even if in our minds they only appear truncated! For example, the idea I currently have that the sun is bigger in the evening than at midday is false if I consider it to be the idea of the sun's size, but as we know, perception envelops two things, the idea of the affection my body undergoes and the idea of the external thing that causes this affection. If I consider the idea that the sun is bigger in the evening than at noon from the angle of the objective truth I lend it as long as I'm ignorant, it's false. But in God, i.e. considered in the whole causal mechanism that produces this idea, it is true, in the sense that the size of the sun cannot appear to me otherwise! Likewise, if I see the stick broken when it's immersed in water, it's a true idea (it follows from Descartes' laws of optics!); it's only false if I say that the stick is really broken, i.e. if I cut the idea from the "fabric" or "weft" of ideas that encompasses it "in God". But the idea "I see the broken stick" is absolutely true.

The explanation comes immediately:

E2P33: There's nothing positive about ideas that would make them false.

The demonstration is clear:

- Suppose a false idea is a reality, then it is a mode of thinking (as are true ideas).

- If it is a reality, it is in God (since everything that is is in God and cannot be conceived without him).

- But in God, all ideas are true.

- So, strictly speaking, misconceptions don't exist. They have no "positive" reality.

We could try to understand this another way. Can we say that there are holes in Gruyère cheese? There are grapes in the grape bread, because grapes exist positively (they are finite modes of infinite substance) whereas the holes in the Gruyère are simply the absence of Gruyère; there is nothing positive in the hole, otherwise we'd be obliged to say that the hole is a mode of existence of nothing!

Proposition XXXIV defines the true idea in us (since in God they are all true, there is no need to define the true idea) as an absolute idea, i.e. adequate and perfect.

Adequate: we already have a definition (D4):

By adequate idea, I mean an idea which, insofar as it is considered in itself, without relation to an object, has all the properties or presents all the intrinsic signs of a true idea.

These are ideas that occur in us in the same way as in God! For example, when I conceive of the circle as the product of the rotation of a segment around one of its extremities, I adequately conceive of the circle. On the other hand, when I don't perceive the Earth's movement and consider it to be immobile, I perceive the Earth only in relation to the effect it has on me, and not absolutely.

It should be noted here that the difference between inadequate and adequate ideas is not the same as Descartes' distinction between confused and clear and distinct ideas. Descartes defines a clear and distinct idea as follows: "[...] knowledge on which an indubitable judgment can be made must be not only clear, but also distinct. I call clear that which is present and manifest to an attentive mind; in the same way that we say that we see hard enough, and that our eyes are disposed to look at them; and distinct, that which is so precise and different from all others, that it includes in itself only that which appears manifest to the one who considers it as it should" (*Principles of Philosophy*, I, 45).

For Descartes, clarity and distinction are produced by a special disposition of the mind. For Spinoza, the situation is quite different. I have an adequate idea of the circle, not because I perceive it clearly and distinctly, but because I perceive the logical sequence of ideas that cause the idea of the circle. When the mind has adequate ideas, it is because it thinks things by their cause. By thinking in this way, the mind thinks for itself—and not, as in thinking by imagination, from the effects of external things on its own body. Thinking by itself, the mind thus thinks freely when and only when it thinks adequately.

We can also now understand what definition IV means when it states that the adequate idea has "all the intrinsic signs" of a true idea: intrinsic, meaning proper to the idea itself and not dependent on something external to the idea. If I define truth as the adequacy of the idea to its object (*adequatio rei et intellectus*), it's an extrinsic "denomination" that I'm using to define the idea as true. Whereas if I consider truth as logical consistency, it's the "intrinsic signs" that allow me to recognize the idea as true.

Proposition XXXV exposes falsity not simply as a deprivation of knowledge, but as a deprivation of knowledge wrapped in inadequate ideas. We return to the idea that falsity arises from the process of knowledge itself. The scolie of this proposition returns to the problem of the illusion of human freedom as ignorance of the causes of actions and awareness of those actions themselves. The appendix to Part I is developed here.

Proposition XXXVI states that there is a causal order to both inadequate and adequate ideas! This is to be expected, if we remember what ideas are. We had an application of this in the appendix to Part I: superstitions appear there as the natural effects of certain inadequate (because partial) ideas: men are born ignorant of causes, but conscious of their appetites.

Common Notions and the Perception of Relationships between Things: The Power of Experience

These three propositions (XXXVII to XXXIX) are devoted to the definition of common notions. First of all, let's avoid any confusion. We are accustomed to calling ideas shared by everyone "common ideas". But the common notions we're talking about here are ideas that represent something common to all bodies. For bodies to agree on certain things, they must have something in common. All bodies have extent and motion in common. Two bodies in particular can have something in common. But what they have in common is not their essence.

Proposition XXXVII is demonstrated by the absurd.

1)   Suppose that something X common to A and B forms the essence of B.

2)   If X forms the essence of B, X cannot be or be conceived without B.

3)   So X can neither be nor be conceived of as forming the essence of A, which is contrary to assumption (1).

At this stage, we can form a vague idea of what these common notions are: being made of metal is something common to the gardener's spade, the kitchen knife and so on. But being made of metal is not the singular essence of any of these things. But one wonders what this is all about. These common things are (since they have an idea that corresponds to them) and are not, since they have no singular reality, existing independently of anything else. So we can explain this: if two things have something in common, it's because they "fit" in a certain respect, i.e. there's a relationship between them. For example, between the spade and the knife there is a relation (of equivalence, i.e. reflexive, symmetrical and transitive), the relation "to be made of the same metal". In short, "common notions" are nothing other than the idea of relationships between things, providing a kind of model of reality.

It is in Proposition XXXVIII that things become a little clearer, since it is asserted that :

E2P38. Things that are common to all and are equally in the part and in the whole can only be adequately conceived.

Let's look at the demonstration. Let us suppose that A is common to all bodies and equally present in the part and in the whole: A therefore belongs to the kind of things defined in E2P37. The idea of A is adequate in God, in accordance with all that we have seen above, since in God there are the ideas of the human body and of the affections of the human body, i.e. those that envelop in part both the nature of the human body and that of the bodies that affect it (cf. *supra*). But sensible perceptions, for example, are adequate in God but inadequate in us, because our minds have only partial and mutilated perceptions: if I don't know the laws of optics, I only perceive a broken stick, but not the causal link between the water, the stick and the path of light that causes me to see the broken stick. But as far as common notions are concerned, I perceive what is common to my body and to bodies, and so here I no longer have a partial and mutilated perception. The idea of what is common is therefore the same in God and in my mind. So it's adequate! In short, the perception of particular things by means of images (the effect of external bodies on my body) is truncated, inadequate, but the perception of relations is adequate, "necessarily" says Spinoza.

Let's go a step further. God produces all extended things (bodies) by giving them common properties—so all bodies are subject to the same laws of motion and rest—here we see clearly how Spinoza is part of the lineage that could be called Galileo and Descartes: all bodies are subject to the principle of inertia, which holds that any body that is not subject to any external force persists in the state in which it finds itself: if it is in motion, it persists in a uniform rectilinear motion, and if it is at rest, it persists at rest (although rest is a uniform rectilinear motion with speed equal to zero!). What all bodies have in common is that they attract each other in proportion to their mass, and inversely in proportion to the square of the distance between their centers of gravity, as Newton showed. But if my mind perceives this kind of relationship, it's not perceiving things that actually exist, in act (the law of gravitation is not something we can perceive, like the apple falling from the tree), it's only perceiving general relationships, common to all bodies. Note that scientific laws

113

are nothing more than general relationships between phenomena—and in no way the knowledge of singular realities, of things in themselves.

We saw with proposition VIII of this part that :

E2P8. The ideas of singular things or non-existent modes must be included in the infinite idea of God in the same way that the formal essences of singular things or modes are contained in the attributes of God.

For example, the idea of something fictitious (e.g. the idea of a house I want to build but which doesn't yet exist outside my mind) is not the idea of something that actually exists. Nevertheless, if I have this idea, it must necessarily be in God, since everything that is is in God and cannot be or be conceived without him. So in God are all the formal essences of things (and ideas are also "things"). In God, then, there are ideas of things that don't actually exist, such as apples, chairs or humans. If I have the idea of general properties, i.e. the relationships between bodies, I'm thinking something that isn't actually there, but is in God as a kind of rule for the production of things—for example, a body cannot be created without it undergoing the law of gravitation. Such rules are not the ideas of a singular thing, of this or that. But when the human mind perceives such common ideas, it perceives the idea exactly as it is "in God".

Proposition XXXVIII has an interesting corollary:

E2P38C. It follows that there are certain ideas, or notions, common to all men.

It's obvious: since men are bodies with common properties, they must all perceive in the same way the kind of adequate ideas that are the common things found in many bodies, in the part and in the whole. Let's translate this: everyone is capable of forming these abstract ideas that describe the most general relationships between bodies, or everyone can learn physics! These common notions are therefore true.

Proposition XXXIX obviously follows from all this: the mind adequately perceives what is common to the human body and other bodies, and by the corollary we see that :

E2P39. It follows that the mind is all the more apt to perceive many things adequately the more its body has in common with other bodies.

Physics in general is all very well. But from this corollary we can conclude that what we can know best is another human being, since we don't agree with any other body as much as with another human body. This little corollary contains within it the whole of Spinoza's *Ethics*. The most perfect knowledge we can have is that of the human mind, and insofar as they know each other adequately, humans agree with each other, and it is only insofar as they know each other inadequately that they are hostile to each other.

Chapter II: "The Nature of the Human Mind", or Mental Reality

The scolie I of proposition XL explains what these common notions are: they are "the foundations of our reasoning". The mind's perception of the relationships between bodies is thus the foundation of reasoning: no longer a question of innate ideas as in classical rationalism (Descartes', for example), but of knowledge that is built up from bodily experiences—Spinoza returns to this in Part Five.

Let's recap and anticipate what's to come:

1)   We have a partial, mutilated knowledge of reality, which is knowledge by "images": external bodies affect our bodies, and this affection is an image of which we have an idea. This way of knowing is inadequate.

2)   However, it is not entirely negative, since we can use this partial knowledge to gain ideas of things common to all bodies. These common notions form a general, abstract knowledge that is not yet the knowledge of singular realities, but it is an adequate knowledge of the general laws of nature, which are the laws of production of reality.

3)   All that remains is to return to the knowledge of singular things based on their laws of production. In other words, a return from abstraction to concreteness, but a concreteness that is no longer an immediate and partial given, but a thought-out concreteness, a synthesis of multiple abstract determinations.

Without forcing the issue, this is an approach found in Hegel (in an idealist form) and in Marx's *Introduction to the Critique of Political Economy*:

"If we started with the population, we'd have a chaotic representation of the whole, and through more precise determination, through analysis, we'd end up with simpler and simpler concepts; from the figurative concrete we'd move on to thinner and thinner abstractions, until we'd arrived at the simplest determinations. From there, we'd have to retrace our steps backwards, until we finally arrived at the population again, but this time not as a chaotic representation of a whole, but as a rich totality of numerous determinations and relationships. The first path is the one taken historically by political economy at its birth. The economists of the seventeenth century, for example, always began with a living totality: population, nation, state, several states; but they always ended by analyzing a few general abstract determining relationships, such as the division of labor, money, value and so on. As soon as these isolated factors have been more or less fixed and abstracted, economic systems have begun, starting with simple notions such as work, division of labor, need, exchange value, and rising to the state, exchanges between nations and the world market. The latter is clearly the correct scientific method. The concrete is concrete because it is the synthesis of multiple determinations, hence the unity of diversity."

The unity of diversity, or the synthesis of multiple determinations, is what knowledge of singular things, based on their laws of production, is all about.

Chapter II: "The Nature of the Human Mind", or Mental Reality

The Three Kinds of Knowledge

From these common notions (adequate ideas), it is possible to deduce other adequate ideas. They are therefore the foundation of science.

The first scolie of proposition XL is a first statement of Spinoza's nominalistic conception, which criticizes *transcendental* terms like Being, Thing, Something. These terms come from the fact that our mind is too limited to conceive simultaneously the images of a great number of things. When there are many bodies, the mind confuses their images under a single attribute. But these terms "signify ideas in the highest degree confused". *Universal notions* (not to be confused with common notions) are born of the same process. For example, by the name of **man,** the mind affirms an infinity of singular beings. These general terms are also confused, and vary according to the most striking features, rather than on the basis of a rigorous definition. (Thus Spinoza recalls the various definitions of man, including this one, which is the subject of a well-known joke: Plato said that man was a featherless biped. His opponents plucked a chicken and sent it to Plato, saying: "Here is a man").

The second scolie is even better known, since it sets out the three kinds of knowledge:

1) Knowledge of the first kind, which groups together knowledge by vague experience and knowledge by signs (or hearsay); this is again knowledge by **Imagination**, which Spinoza has already amply defined.

2)   Knowledge of common notions and adequate ideas about things. This corresponds to scientific knowledge. This is what Spinoza calls **Reason**.

3)   The third kind of knowledge alone possesses the name of **Science**. But it is an **intuitive** science. It is knowledge that starts from God and goes to the essence of things.

Knowledge of the first kind is the only cause of falsity, knowledge of the other two kinds being true (E2P41), consequently (E2P42) it is knowledge of kinds 2 and 3 that allows us to distinguish truth from falsity. Finally, proposition XLIII affirms the self-evidence of truth:

E2P43. He who has a true idea knows at the same time that he has a true idea, and cannot doubt the truth of the thing.

Why is this so? The scolie of this proposition rests on the idea that the true is its own norm and the norm of the false. Let's see what this means. We could sum up Spinoza's proposition (E2P43D) in another way: "He who knows a thing truly, must at the same time have an adequate idea of his knowledge." To understand the demonstration, which, like all demonstrations, is a little rough, it's best to go through the scolie. This states that the preceding proposition is "sufficiently manifest by itself". To have a true idea is to know a thing "perfectly or as well as possible", and no one can doubt this, says Spinoza, unless we take an idea as something mute, "like a painting on a blackboard and not a mode of thinking". To understand this, we need to return to the refutation of the conception of truth as the agreement of the idea and its object. If the true idea is true through agreement with its object, it has, says Spinoza, no more reality than the false idea! Let's imagine the idea as a painting. Take, for example, the best-known portrait of Machiavelli by Santo di Tito. This portrait was painted several decades after Machiavelli's death. It may look very much like him, or it may not look like him at all. It's impossible to know for sure: the likeness of Machiavelli's portrait to the Florentine secretary is undecidable. On the other hand, when I have the idea of the sum of the three angles of a triangle, I know what mental operations I have carried out, and I know that it is necessarily worth two right angles: demonstrations are the eyes of the mind. Nothing is more certain than a true idea! Hence this beautiful statement:

E2P43S. Just as light makes itself and darkness appear, so truth is its own standard and that of falsehood.

Adequate Knowledge. Why We are not Doomed to Wander in the Dark

The propositions that follow then set out the principles of adequate knowledge. Everything now seems clear.

According to Proposition XL, reason, by nature, regards things as necessary. If we perceive them as contingent, it's because we're missing a link in our reasoning. Chance in nature is merely the fruit of our ignorance. This question lies at the heart of the discussion surrounding the "Copenhagen interpretation" of quantum physics. For Heisenberg, the uncertainty surrounding exact knowledge of the electron is ontological: nature is non-deterministic at the microphysical level, an interpretation that Einstein always rejected: "*Gott würfelt nicht*" ("God doesn't play dice"). Apparent indeterminism must be explained by "hidden variables", Einstein always maintained. In any case, if we perceive things as contingent, this is the result of knowledge by imagination (knowledge of the first kind).

The corollary of proposition XLIV is that things must be perceived *sub quaedam aeternitatis specie* when they are perceived by reason. If things are perceived as necessary indeed, which is how we must perceive them when we are in the knowledge of the second or third kind, then they are perceived under the aspect of God's eternal necessity. For example, if I don't understand a natural phenomenon, I consider it contingent. But as soon as I know its causes, i.e.

as soon as I have understood it on the basis of the general laws under which all things are produced, this phenomenon is no longer perceived as temporally determined (here and now) but as destined to recur at any time as long as the causes are brought together. When I grasp the fall of a body from the knowledge of Galileo's law, it's not the body that falls here at such and such a time in such and such a place, it's a manifestation of $x = -1/2\ gt^2$! In this formula, time itself is transformed into a kind of eternal variable.

Here again, let's anticipate: the more I know things adequately, the more I grasp them under a species of eternity, and therefore the more my mind participates in eternity, which is why Spinoza could say: "We feel and experience that we are eternal" (E5P23S).

Every idea of a singular thing envelops the eternal essence of God, asserts proposition XLV. Here again, it's obvious: every idea of a thing derives from the mode of production of that thing. If I look at this little bacterium under the microscope, this bacterium has been produced by a set of infinite causes, and the ideas of these causes, linking up in order, are in God, and consequently in the idea that in this bacterium is included in some respect the eternal essence of God. We find the same thing in Leibniz in another form, when he says that each monad expresses the whole of creation.

Consequence: knowledge of singular things, existing in act (and not knowledge of the effects of things on our bodies), is knowledge of God. This is knowledge of the third kind, which in Part V will be called "intellectual love of God". This is what Proposition XLVI affirms: "The knowledge of the eternal and infinite essence of God that every idea envelops is adequate and perfect." Nothing more to say. Knowledge by reason leads to this: knowledge of God, "adequate and perfect". This is what proposition XLVII states. But this is not a knowledge reserved for the philosopher who has studied long and hard. The scolie specifies: "The infinite essence of God and his eternity are known to all." In other words, no one can really err. Our imagination can blur what we see clearly, but it can never really prevent our mind from seeing what is. Indeed, rather than clinging to what we know about God's essence, we try to imagine him as we imagine Peter or Paul. And, by the way, it's hard to avoid imagining him in this way, since our bodies are constantly subject to the affects of external things. One of the major causes of the blurring of this perception is the kind of knowledge that comes from the equivocal signs of words. Spinoza's example is quite clear. If I say that the straight lines passing through the center of a circle are unequal, it's because the word circle is not understood in the sense of mathematicians, and that in reality I call an ellipse, for example, a "circle". But in his perception of his mind, nobody can say that a figure constituted by the rotation of a diameter could have unequal diameters. Long before Wittgenstein, Spinoza asserted that no one can think illogically; one can only speak equivocally, incomprehensible

Chapter II: "The Nature of the Human Mind", or Mental Reality

to others, or stammer meaningless phrases, but one cannot think illogically.

Intellect and Will: Why there is no Faculty of Will

The last two propositions (XLVIII and XLIX) are devoted to establishing that the free will does not exist; the will in its operation is not distinct from the understanding (proposition XLVIII). The faculties of the soul are pure fictions, metaphysical beings, universals. Here again, we have a reprise of Spinozist nominalism: there are only modes of thinking, all singular.

The long scolie of proposition XLIX that closes this second part deserves to be analyzed in detail. In it, we find the essential idea in Spinoza's thought that error is nothing positive, but merely a deprivation of knowledge. False ideas are never frankly false: they are truncated or confused ideas. The drunkard who claims to have seen pink elephants is not, strictly speaking, mistaken. He has seen pink elephants—the state of his brain has produced this image—but he lacks the knowledge that pink elephants don't exist. The true idea envelops certainty, while the false idea does not. Spinoza makes it clear that we must not confuse "not doubting" with "having certainty".

First of all, says Spinoza, we must carefully distinguish between images, ideas and words. Confusing these three terms leads to a failure to understand the true doctrine of the will. Now, says Spinoza, an idea is not a mute painting on a panel. In other words, an idea is not a copy in the mind of the thing perceived. Strictly speaking, it is not a "representation". An idea has as its cause another idea, and produces as its effect one or more other ideas. An idea is an act, not something passive. It is the very act of understanding: to understand is to form ideas. The basic error is to confuse the idea, which is of the order of thought, with images and words, which, being bodily movements, are of the order of extent. Spinoza reviews the objections to his thesis. These objections are all based on the inner evidence of the will and our ability to suspend judgment—a Cartesian thesis. Spinoza shows that this inner self-evidence is an illusion, and that the ability to suspend judgment is not the result of free will but of inadequate knowledge.

The fundamental sources of error are finally identified: we easily err when we confuse general notions with singular ones, beings of reason and abstractions with real things.

The end of the scolie is devoted to showing that this doctrine is justified by its usefulness for life since:
- It gives peace of mind in every respect.
- It teaches how to deal with chance.
- It's good for social life.
- It teaches how to conceive the government of men.
- This conclusion paves the way for the following parts.

The "reform of the understanding", to use the title of one of Spinoza's unfinished works, leads to knowledge, and

Chapter II: "The Nature of the Human Mind", or Mental Reality

knowledge is key to Spinoza's morality and politics. A proper understanding of reality enables us to dispel vain fears and become good citizens. It is clear, then, that the *Ethics* is entirely oriented towards these practical goals: it is not an abstract metaphysics or a pure theory of knowledge.

Chapter III:
Genesis and Classification of Feelings

To recap: the first part of the *Ethics deals* with the nature of things, all of which derive from an eternal, infinite reality with an infinite number of attributes, each of which expresses an eternal, infinite essence. The second part, on the nature of the mind, establishes that the mind is nothing other than the idea of the body, and shows the conditions under which we can have adequate ideas, elevating us from the first to the third kind of knowledge, i.e. from spontaneous knowledge by imagination to intuitive knowledge of singular essences, via knowledge of natural laws, based on "common notions". It now remains to get to the heart of the matter, that is, the core of the work as defined by its title.

What are ethics? Greek *ethos* refers to morals (what the Latins call *mores*), the more or less explicit standards of common life. When ancient philosophers—Aristotle, for example—constructed an ethic, they were concerned with defining the general ends of human life and the means to achieve these ends. An ethic thus has a descriptive part (what is the human soul, how is it affected, what can it do?) and a normative part. Spinoza's Ethics meets these requirements. It includes a general theory of the affections of the soul or sentiments (essentially in Part III). Part IV examines what the human soul can and cannot do, and sketches out a moral framework. Finally, Part V defines the sovereign good, bliss.

Part III consists of a preamble, a first part up to proposition XI that establishes the foundations of the affective life, a second part (from proposition XII to LVII) that explores the maze of the life of feelings, and a brief final part that deals with "the feelings that relate to us as we are active".

Preamble: For a Rational Study of the Human Mind. Controversy with Descartes

The preamble is both a summary of what has been learned in Part II, and an outline of the method to be followed in studying the genesis of affections of the mind and the complex relationships that characterize their actual existence in the human mind.

In line with all that has been established above, this involves considering "human feelings and conduct" as "natural things". Spinoza criticizes the conception of man as an "empire within an empire". Man does not disturb the order of nature, but follows its course. Crucial point: to those who oppose the human world to the natural world, human freedom to natural necessity, human artifice to things that arise naturally, Spinoza answers unambiguously: everything human is as natural as all other natural things. We'll see it again later: morality and political institutions are not "unnatural" devices, but can only proceed from natural laws, and nothing can be established that is unnatural.

Thus, human impotence and inconstancy have their cause in nature, and not in some vice of human nature about which we should whine. This is followed by a scathing critique of the "moralists", who more often than not content themselves with detesting the vices of the mind: [...] "whoever can most eloquently or subtly indict the impotence of the human mind passes for divine." On the contrary, Spinoza advises the wise man to extol man's power at every opportunity.

Spinoza notes that "the very illustrious Descartes", despite his theory of free will, sought to explain the passions of the soul ("human feelings") by their first causes and, at the same time, wanted to show how the will can have absolute empire over feelings. But this attempt failed. We must show how vices are themselves necessary products of Nature. We must therefore deal with the vices and futility of men "according to the geometrical method", "by rigorous reasoning", as if it were a question of "lines, planes or bodies".

Chapter III: Genesis and Classification of Feelings

Definitions and Postulates

The definitions set the stage for our treatment of human feelings and behavior. They extend the definitions in Part II.

Adequate cause: as we have seen, an adequate idea is one that is in me as it is in God; I know its objective explanation. An adequate cause is, similarly, one whose effect can be clearly and distinctly perceived by itself.

To be active: something happens of which we are the adequate cause. To be active, then, is to act in accordance with a clear knowledge of the laws of nature, and not to act blindly, under the sway of external forces of which we have only a vague knowledge. On the contrary, we are **passive** when something happens within us, or when something follows from our nature, of which we are only the *partial cause*. There's no need to "intellectualize" too much. To live, man must have a certain number of adequate ideas that drive his actions. He needs a varied diet to replace the various parts that make up his body. But he is only partially responsible for his own actions when he falls into bulimia or drunkenness. Note here the strange formulas for those steeped in the philosophies of the subject. "It happens", "it follows" something of our nature, says Spinoza. It is not the "I" that is the absolute origin of all this. Not this original "I" detached from the world (not this Cartesian "I-God"), no! "It happens. It's an impersonal phenomenon: a feeling or a behavior, and the sum total of all these things that occur gives us the "I" (an expression that Spinoza doesn't use). But the "me" is only a result, caught up in the flow of things that happen to me, i.e. things that involve the parts that make me up. This is the furthest thing from the thinking of the "illustrious Descartes".

Feelings (or affects): these are "affections of the body" that modify its power to act, and at the same time, the ideas of these affections. In other words, feelings are things that occur in the body, and which necessarily have a corresponding idea in the mind, since the mind is the idea of the body, and therefore includes the ideas of the body's affections. Affection and the idea of that affection are one and the same thing, "at the same time", as Spinoza puts it. This definition of feelings can be applied to the classification of active and passive states. Affections for which we are the adequate causes are actions, and those for which we are not the adequate causes are passions. We can ourselves be the adequate cause of our feelings, which may derive from our own nature and not from the action on us of extraneous causes. We'll see (E3P58-59) what these active feelings are, and how the mind can self-affect.

Two postulates follow these definitions, both of which concern the body. Postulate I asserts that the human body can be affected in "many ways", either increasing, decreasing or leaving equal the power to act. Bodies act on each other and obey the laws of physics. This is why feelings are natural things that can be understood according to the order of nature. Postulate II (which in fact follows on from what

Chapter III: Genesis and Classification of Feelings

we have already seen in E2) indicates that the body can keep track of the changes it has undergone (these are the impressions of the objects whose affections it has undergone).

Fundamental Propositions: Action and Passion. The Relationship Between Body and Mind

Proposition I is quite obvious:

E3P1. Our mind is partly active, but partly passive, namely: insofar as it has adequate ideas, it is necessarily active, and insofar as it has inadequate ideas, it is necessarily passive.

Of course, this is true for "us", i.e. for all humans. Our minds are partly active, partly passive. There will surely be a gradation between those whose minds are composed of a maximum of adequate ideas and those who have almost no adequate ideas (cf. corollary). But no one is entirely passive. Anyone who was entirely passive would soon die! As for being entirely active, that's just as impossible, because the most learned of scholars, the wisest of sages, has a body, and his body will collide with other bodies that will affect him in such a way that his power to act will be affected. Spinoza's body was affected by Koch's bacillus (as far as we know), which eventually took its toll on the dead sage aged just over 44.

Proposition II states that there is no relationship between mind and body. The body cannot determine the mind to think, and the mind cannot determine the body to move. There is no causal link between body and mind, which we already knew from the start when the definition of the finite thing in its kind teaches us that a thing can only be limited by a thing of the same kind. Attributes cannot have anything in common. We call this Spinozist affirmation "the affirmation of parallelism". This parallelism asserts that mind and body are always simultaneously (*simul*) affected or acting, because they both express the same essence. But we must be wary of the expression "parallelism", as it implies two different lines that are somehow linked together by a mysterious force that guarantees the maintenance of this parallelism. But in truth, for Spinoza, these two lines are not different: they are the same thing considered under two different attributes. A depressive does not have a depressive psychic state parallel to his physical state (dysregulation of the neurotransmitter serotonin).

The Important Skolion of Proposition II: Mind and Body are One and the Same

If mind and body have no relation, it's simply because the idea of relation would refer to two different things. Now, the scolie of Proposition II states:

E3P2S. Spirit and Body are one and the same thing, conceived sometimes under the attribute of thought, sometimes under that of extent.

It follows that :

The order of actions and passions of our Body corresponds, by nature, to the order of actions and passions of the Spirit.

This is obvious from E2P12, which states that "whatever happens in the object of the idea constituting the human mind must be perceived by the human mind". Put another way: what happens in the body is perceived in the mind. But Spinoza is not content to resort to demonstration. As always, experience is our most powerful aid. This scolie contains most of the arguments that the materialists of the following century (Diderot and d'Holbach) would use, first and foremost, to refute Cartesian dualism.

First experimental argument: "No one has determined what the body can do [...]". We invoke the action of the mind on the body precisely because we know nothing serious about the body and, lacking knowledge, we resort as usual to one of these "asylums of ignorance" arguments. Spinoza rejects conceptions of the body as something passive that needs to be "animated". He points out that what we observe in beasts is "far beyond human sagacity." Note that this is an argument found, for other purposes, in Montaigne (*Apologie de Raymond*

Sebon) or Charron, and is typically an anti-Cartesian argument—revealing in this respect is the anonymous manuscript on *Le Sentiment des bêtes* (Douai library) studied by Olivier Bloch in his work on clandestine literature: the question of the thought of beasts directly raises the question of the nature of the human mind. Another argument, equally anti-Cartesian, is that of the somnambulist: somnambulists perform acts in their sleep that they would not dare to do awake.

> *This proves that the Body, by the laws of its nature alone, can do many things that its Spirit remains astonished by.*

So the idea that the actions of the body can be explained by the decrees of the mind is nothing more than a way of camouflaging ignorance, to be equated with the "will of God", that asylum of ignorance referred to in the first part.

> *Hence it follows that men, when they say that such and such an action of the Body has its origin in the Spirit, which has empire over the Body, do not know what they are saying and thus only confess in specious terms that they are ignorant of the true cause of an action and are not surprised by it.*

Once again Spinoza attacks the illusions of consciousness. We believe it is in our power to act, speak or remain silent, in short we are aware that the decrees of the mind command the body—just as we believe ourselves to be free because we are aware of our desires and unaware of the real causes that make us desire (cf. appendix to E1). Relying on experience, Spinoza reverses the order of the illusions of consciousness (exactly as he does in the appendix to Part I, which this scolie seems in many parts to echo). For it is obvious that :

> *If the Body is inert, the Spirit is at the same time incapable of thinking. For when the Body is at rest during sleep, the Spirit is asleep with it, and has no power to think in the waking state.*

We know that the mind thinks when the body is asleep (it dreams), but it's a thought of a sleeping body, which merely stirs up the body's internal states and the images imprinted on it (cf. postulate), and in no way a waking thought. Here, then, is experimental proof that the mind has no power independent of the body. Opposing this is an argument that could be described as materialistic: proponents of the theory of the mind independent of the body and having power over it object that the body alone could not produce all the sophisticated works of human culture, to which Spinoza replies that we "don't know what the body can or what can be deduced from its nature", and yet:

> *Experience teaches us that by the laws of Nature alone, a great many things happen that we would never have believed could happen without the guidance of Spirit...*

Here again, it's obvious. Humans are capable of making very powerful computers, but incapable of artificially producing even a very crude protozoan. So a protozoa is a more complex thing than a computer, and it is produced by the laws of nature alone, without involving the decree of the human mind. The very structure of the human mind, says Spinoza, "in skill far surpasses anything produced by human art". It's worth noting that underlying this is Spinozist thinking about man's limits. "From Nature considered under any attribute, follow an infinity of things". From man undoubtedly follows only a finite number of things. The power of nature infinitely surpasses the power of man, and the complexity of nature infinitely surpasses anything that a human brain can think, a brain itself so complex that it far surpasses what human artifice can do, as experience, centuries after Spinoza, continues to show. It's perhaps only a short step from there to perceiving in Spinoza a sense of man's disproportion to nature, not so far removed from Pascal's sense of man's disproportion to the universe, which we should try to cross one day. In any case, it's not Spinoza who would use human science and technology to make us "like masters and possessors of nature" (cf. Descartes, *Discourse on Method*, Part VI).

The second objection is a return to human freedom, i.e. to a question that has already been settled, and which is taken up again here from a different angle. Once again, experience shows us our inability to control our appetites. Once again,

Spinoza recalls the ordinary beliefs that come from the data of our immediate consciousness:

I agree, human affairs would go much better if it were equally in man's power to keep silent or to speak. But experience shows enough and beyond that men have nothing less in their power than their tongues, and that they can do nothing less than regulate their desires; whence most believe that we act freely only with regard to things we desire moderately, because the desire for these things may be easily thwarted by the recollection of something else we often remember; but that we are not at all free with regard to things we desire with a lively affection that the recollection of something else cannot appease. But, in truth, if they did not know from experience that we perform more than one act which we then repent of, and that often—for example when we are divided by contrary feelings—we see the best and follow the worst, nothing would prevent them from believing that we always act freely.

Once again, experience is the only way to curb the illusion of freedom born in our immediate consciousness.

Experience itself therefore teaches, no less clearly than Reason, that men believe themselves to be free for the sole reason that they are conscious of their actions and ignorant of the causes by which they are determined; it further shows that the decrees of the mind are nothing apart from the

*appetites themselves, and are therefore variable according to
the variable state of the Body.*

And so

*The decree of the Spirit as well as the appetite and deter-
mination of the Body go together by nature, or rather are one
and the same thing we call Decree.*

The so-called "will" is nothing more than a name for the
body's appetites. It is not "determined" by the body's appetites
(which would imply that it has an independent existence);
it is the same thing. Here, Nietzsche could be compared
to Spinoza. Nietzsche's ontology is monistic. We have no
"*given*" other than appetites and passions. We must therefore
understand the material world as a unity from which we do
not differ. It's a question of method that Nietzsche invokes.
There's no point in assuming many separate causes in advance.
The method is to try to find just one, to reduce the diverse to
a single principle, "to the point of absurdity", he says.

Thus, the body must be conceived as a "field of forces",
the combination and opposition of drives: if the human body
is an individual composed of a large number of individuals,
themselves highly composed (cf. E2), each of these individuals
has its own *conatus*, its own effort to persevere in its being, and
the effort of the human body as a whole is the result of this.
And the material world in general is not substantially different.

139

It only appears as a more primitive form. Complication and combination of systems of forces: such is life, and this is why the world "seen from within" appears as the *will to power* and nothing else. This definition eliminates the traditional metaphysical concept of will. "There is no will", Nietzsche repeats (see *Beyond Good and Evil*). By reducing the "will to power" to the interplay of forces in our world, it is the will as a metaphysical substance or faculty of the subject that disappears.

There is no will, because the human "will" is not some mysterious faculty that precedes action, but the result (the resultant, according to the parallelogram rule of forces) of the contradictory combinations of tendencies, of drives struggling with each other for preponderance. What we call will is merely the temporary triumph of one drive over the others, or the translation into conscious terms of the temporary state of equilibrium that has been established in the interplay of drives. The will to power is simply the deployment of forces, unfinalized and without any predetermined goal. Life, and *a fortiori* human life, is but a special case of the will to power, which, as Nietzsche says, diversifies, refines and also weakens.

Let's return to Spinoza. The conclusion of this development of the scolie of Proposition II of Part Three is that belief in the will is a dream:

Those who believe that they speak, remain silent or do anything by virtue of a free decree of the Spirit are dreaming with their eyes open.

The formulation is obviously highly ironic, since it comes at the end of an analysis of memory and dreaming.

Action and Passion

Proposition III reaffirms the correspondence between action and passion, adequate ideas and inadequate ideas. To make himself clear, he specifies that:

> *E3P3S. The passions relate to the mind only insofar as it contains something that envelops a negation, in other words insofar as it is regarded as a part of Nature that cannot be perceived clearly and distinctly by itself and apart from others.*

Let's try to make sense of this terse and somewhat enigmatic explanation. Firstly, passions relate to the mind "only as", i.e. only when the mind is considered from a certain angle. If there is passion, it's because the mind contains something that envelops a negation. A mind contains ideas (since it is itself an idea), and an idea that envelops a negation is an inadequate idea, i.e. a truncated idea. Why does the mind contain such ideas? Simply because it is only a part of nature, and cannot be perceived in itself, "apart from others". Man is not a cause of himself, and he cannot exist apart from all the relationships with the other natural things on which his life depends, and so his mind cannot be conceived in itself, and so always contains ideas that envelop a negation.

From this we can deduce two important propositions which, however, Spinoza does not explicitly deduce:

1° It is therefore by nature that man is subject to the passions, and so a man without passion, a man devoted exclusively to following Reason, simply doesn't exist. We'll see that the thought of death is inadequate, but it's hard to see how a human being can concern himself exclusively with the meditation of life. Even the wisest of Spinozist sages must sometimes think about his own death, without being able to think about it. Here again, there may be an insurmountable barrier, a new expression of Spinoza's philosophy of the limit.

2° The human mind is inconceivable "apart from others". If I call the idea I have of my own mind "me" (since we've known since E2 that the mind is an idea that also contains "the idea of the idea"), then the "me" is inconceivable apart from other minds, which also contain a "me". And so the detached self, the pure interiority that Western philosophy from Augustine to Descartes and from Descartes to Kant is after, is an inadequate idea. It is at its core that the idealist philosophy of the subject is undermined.

Effort or Conatus. Basic Relations in the Physics of Feelings

Propositions IV to VIII define the essence of a thing by its effort to persevere in its being. Thus proposition IV:

E3P4. Nothing can be destroyed, except by an external cause.

Indeed, if essence does not envelop existence (except the essence of substance), neither can it envelop non-existence. Just as a thing is born (comes into existence) under the effect of an external thing that causes it, so it can only disappear under the effect of an external cause: no man can be born other than by the meeting of his parents' gametes in the maternal uterus, and death is always the effect of an external cause, whether accidental death, illness or the general wear and tear of the body confronted with other bodies. This is why existence is indefinite, since the finitude of a thing is not its essence. This helps us to understand Proposition VIII:

E3P8. The effort by which everything strives to persevere in its being envelops no finite time, but indefinite time.

Proposition V states that things are contrary when one can destroy the other. Two ideas that contradict each other destroy each other, and two extended things that contradict each other destroy each other. For Spinoza, contradiction is a serious but devastating thing.

These negative definitions pave the way for the positive definition.

> *E3P6. Each thing, according to its power of being, strives to persevere in its being.*

And Proposition VII:

> *E3P7. The effort by which each thing strives to persevere in its being is nothing outside the actual essence of that thing.*

Effort is generally translated from the Latin *conatus* (Appuhn, Caillois, for example). This word also designates the impulse, the instinctive tendency. We could translate the German *Trieb* as "impulse", if we don't mind pulling Spinoza too close to Freud. What is this effort? The *European Vocabulary of Philosophers* superbly ignores *conatus*. The Larousse dictionary of philosophy devotes a note to it. *Conatus* is first referred to in Hobbes' *De Corpore*, where it designates the instantaneous state of a body that includes a tendency to move. From a material point of view, we could say that *conatus is* its impulse-vector. This impulse-vector is conserved in an isolated system, but it can also be composed with others. In a still incomplete form, this is what we find in Cartesian physics (cf. Descartes, *Principles of Philosophy*, II), and it's another formulation of the principle of inertia that Galileo had first formulated. We can therefore assume that this is what Spinoza has in mind. But this representation of the *conatus is undoubtedly* insufficient. Being strives to persevere in its being. We have seen (cf. E2) that an individual is a compound body that maintains the relationships between its component parts, and that, to this end, can integrate external parts into its own structure to replace worn-out parts, or to make the component parts grow (without substantially changing the relationships). *Conatus*, then, could be the principle of structural maintenance that characterizes all individuals (the living). Finally, *conatus* could be translated as "drive" in the sense of Freudian *eros*. But here, there is no *thanatos*, no death drive—for Spinoza, a death drive would be as inconceivable as a square circle.

A second important idea needs to be explained: everything strives to persevere in its being, but "according to its power to be". God possesses absolute power (*potentia*), but he has no power (*potestas*), since God does not act according to his pleasure like a capricious tyrant. Man, then, being a finite mode of infinite power, possesses only finite power. As the amoeba is also a finite mode, it too has a finite power. So it is with all finite beings. Their essence is nothing other than their power to exist, which can be greater or lesser. Every being exists in accordance with its power to exist, which is nothing other than the power to act in accordance with its own nature. Nothing could be easier to understand. But a being can be and is affected by other beings. These affections modify this power to exist. Those who are under the influence of sad passions see their power to exist diminish: the man who is unhappy because he has lost his loved one no longer enjoys anything. Sadness always lowers vital energy.

Proposition IX applies what has just been said about all "things" in general to human minds. The mind strives to persevere in its being as much in so far as it has clear and distinct ideas as in so far as it has confused ideas. Note that it is also in so far as it has confused ideas that the human mind tends to persevere in its being. Even if it is mistaken as to the reality of its conduct, the human being always seeks to persevere in its being. So the essence of the mind is made up of adequate ideas (sources of action) and inadequate ideas (sources of passions). The will, insofar as this term retains any meaning, is the mind's effort to persevere in its being when it relates to the mind alone. When it refers to the mind and body, this effort is called "appetite". Consequence: appetite is the essence of man, an appetite that can still be called "Desire" when it is conscious of itself. The Spinozist definition makes man a being of desire. The scolie of Proposition IX sums up the Spinozist doctrine. Human beings, like all other beings, are determined by the effort (*conatus*) to persevere in their being. This effort is called will when it relates to the mind alone, and appetite when it relates to both mind and body.

E3P9S. Appetite is therefore nothing other than the very essence of man, and from the nature of this essence necessarily follow the things that serve its preservation. [...] Desire is Appetite accompanied by self-consciousness.

It should be noted that desire is not fixed *a priori* on specific goals that would steer it in this or that direction. We may wonder what is meant by the definition of Desire as Appetite with Consciousness. It's important to understand that consciousness adds nothing to appetite. Desire is simply self-conscious appetite, which again imposes itself by virtue of the fact that the mind possesses the ideas of bodily affections and the ideas of these ideas.

We must also link this definition to the scolie of Proposition II, in which Spinoza sets out in detail, as we have seen, the thesis of the illusion of free will. The consciousness that accompanies desire is not an adequate knowledge of the causes that impel us to act, but only an awareness of the objects to which appetite is directed. It is therefore a vague, truncated consciousness. From this stem a number of conclusions that, at first glance, may offend traditional moralism. Thus, good and bad are determined by this fundamental effort:

E3P9S. It is therefore established by all that precedes that we do not make an effort towards any thing, that we do not want it, and do not tend towards it by appetite or desire, because we judge it to be good; it is the opposite: we judge a thing to be good, because we make an effort towards it, that we want it and tend towards it by appetite or desire.

Let's sum it up even more succinctly: we don't desire something because it's good, but on the contrary, we consider it good because we desire it. This is why we can desire things that are very bad in themselves, because they are contrary to the nature of our body or mind, but which we find good because we desire them. All the mechanisms of passionate illusion are here in their nascent form.

Proposition X is almost self-evident:

E3P10. An idea that excludes the existence of our Body cannot be in our Spirit, but is contrary to it.

An easy experiment: I can't imagine myself dead! I can imagine others mourning my death (or rejoicing in it). I can imagine my body dead, but I can't imagine myself non-existent. The reason is simple and purely logical: since the mind is the idea of the body, it cannot contain an idea that excludes the idea of the body. Here, as always, we find the strict identity in the difference between being and being-conceived.

The demonstration includes the positive correlate of this proposition:

[...] since what first and foremost constitutes the essence of the Spirit is the idea of the body existing in act, what is first

and foremost in our mind is the effort to affirm the existence of our Body [...].

The idea of our spirit without the body is pure nonsense, and the spirit's first concern is to affirm the existence of the body. This is the antithesis of a certain (more or less Manichean) Christianity, which sees the salvation of the soul only in the contempt of the body. And obviously, if there is no spirit without a body, there can be no place for an immortal soul!

The relationship (if we can use this term) between mind and body is not one that the mind undergoes passively. In the Cartesian treatise *Passions de l'âme*, passion is the (generally bad) influence of "animal spirits" on the soul, since it produces ideas that envelop both body and soul, and therefore confused ideas. For Spinoza, the most important thing for the mind is to express the power of the body. No two positions could be more antagonistic.

This way of positing human reality as a "body-mind" is reinforced and clarified in Proposition XI:

E3P11. From what increases or decreases, helps or hinders our Body's power to act, the idea increases or decreases, helps or hinders our Spirit's power to think.

In other words, the healthier the body, the better the mind can think: *mens sana in corpore sano,* as the Latins would say, following in the footsteps of the Greeks. The power to think and the power to act are more than correlated. They are the same thing, conceived in two different ways.

The scolie of this proposition is yet another of the knots ordering the work as a whole. We must stop here. In this scolie, Spinoza defines the fundamental laws of changes in the state of the mind, the laws that control variations in "vital tone". The mind "can undergo great changes, and pass sometimes to a greater perfection, but sometimes to a lesser; and these passions explain to us the feelings of Joy and Sadness".

Perfection is existence itself. But as we've seen, we can increase or decrease our power to exist (or the effort to persevere in our being), and consequently our perfection can increase or decrease. Obviously, there's no moral connotation here. Joy is an increase in the power to act, an increase in "vital tonus", and sadness a decrease in the power to act. It's all very easy to understand. A cheerful person is in top form, and nothing stands in his way; a depressed person, on the other hand, is downcast, and the slightest difficulty becomes an ordeal. Experience confirms the accuracy of Spinoza's propositions. Spinoza then breaks down these passions, when they relate to both body and mind, into "titillation" or gaiety and pain or melancholy (the former applies to the body locally, while the latter applies to the whole body).

We now have the definition of the three primary feelings: desire, joy, sadness. To understand the rest, we need to get to grips with the Spinozist "topic". The primary layer of feeling is the *conatus*. The elementary feelings of joy and sadness express modifications of the *conatus*. In practice, primary feelings are never pure. In practice, they are always closely intertwined and, above all, appear linked to an imagined object. These elementary feelings thus appear as "rational abstractions" from which the complexity of human feelings and behaviour can be reconstructed by thought. This is the subject of the following propositions.

With this in mind, Spinoza returns to proposition X and what is meant by an idea contrary to another. We are reminded that the present existence of our spirit depends on this alone: "the spirit envelops the present existence of the body" (no dualism, then, no soul separate from the body... And no immortality of the soul!). Similarly, the power of the mind (which enables it to imagine and remember, cf. E2P14-15-16) also depends on its enveloping the existence of the body. So as soon as the mind ceases to assert the existence of the body, it loses all power and thus ceases to imagine, remember, etc. But such a situation cannot come from the mind itself, since that would mean that the mind contains within itself the principle of its own destruction, which would be contrary to E3P4. But since a thing can only be limited by a thing of the same nature, it is not the destruction of the body that produces the destruction of the mind either: it must therefore be another idea that contradicts the idea of our body as mind, and therefore an idea that excludes the present existence of the body.

Chapter III: Genesis and Classification of Feelings

The Confusion of Feelings

This title, borrowed from a short story by Stefan Zweig published in 1927, is the perfect way to describe what Spinoza is trying to unravel in propositions XII to XLII. It's both a genealogy and a classification system for feelings, in the knowledge that they always appear entangled in the same individual, and that the mind is always in that state of oscillation that Spinoza calls "the fluctuations of the soul".

The imaginary fixation of desire

We have seen that desire is one of the three primary feelings. This desire, as an appetite, proceeds from the *conatus*, whose strength it manifests. But this desire is never fixed in advance. It is a desire for X, with any X filling the void as circumstances dictate. Here's Proposition XII:

> *E3P12. The Spirit, as much as it can, strives to imagine what increases or helps the Body's power to act.*

Imagination plays a central role here. We saw in Part Two how it leads to inadequate ideas. The affections of the mind are caused by inadequate ideas, and imagination envelops inadequate ideas. Imagination is therefore always linked to affections. But imagination is not something external to the natural movement of the mind. Quite the contrary, in fact. The mind strives as hard as it can," says Spinoza. Imagination, then, is an expression of the *conatus,* and plays a part in the affective life.

Proposition XIII completes the previous one:

E3P13. When the Spirit imagines things that diminish or prevent the Body's power to act, it strives, as much as it can, to remember the things that exclude the existence of the former.

And the corollary:
Hence the mind's reluctance to imagine anything that diminishes or opposes its power and that of the body.

From here, we immediately arrive at the definitions of the first "object" or 1st-order feelings. (Primary feelings can indeed be described as zero-order feelings. They can be qualified in themselves, and don't need an object to be conceived. Pure joy or sadness without reason, we know roughly what that means). We'll call feelings that are fixed on an object "1st order feelings". We'll justify this name more clearly later, when we move on to feelings of order 2, and so on. So the first feelings fixed on objects are love and hate. They are respectively joy and sadness linked to an object. Love is joy accompanied by the idea of an external cause, and sadness is hatred accompanied by the idea of an external cause. As the mind strives to maintain or increase its power, and joy is an increase in the power to act, it will therefore strive to keep present the thing it loves, and to destroy the thing it hates.

What we need to remember from these two propositions is that, in the traditional conception, love is the lover's will to unite with the beloved. Love thus derives from judgment (it is the result of an intentional action). For Spinoza, this proposition renders love incomprehensible, or to be more precise, reverses the real order, and causes what is merely a derivative effect to be taken as the cause. If the lover wants to unite with the thing he loves, it is precisely because he loves it by virtue of joy, i.e. by virtue of an exaltation of his own power of being that he experiences with the accompaniment of the imagination of this thing. Joy, i.e. the personal enjoyment of our own power to be, is the basis of the impulse to love.

Conclusion 1: we don't love something because we judge it to be good, but we judge it to be good because we love it. That's why love is blind!

Conclusion 2: Spinoza, long before Freud, demystifies love. Demystification in the literal sense of the word (removing mystical masks), but not the kind of depreciation that misanthropes are wont to utter.

Explaining the mechanisms of desire fixation

Propositions XIV and XV explain how desire is accidentally fixed on a particular object, using the mechanism of association (cf. E2P18 on associations of ideas). Proposition XV specifies that a thing can, by accident, be the cause of joy, sadness or desire. Our sentimental relations are therefore without serious reason (in substance), but result from the clash of bodies and the combination of old events in our minds. Thus the corollary of E3P15C:

E3P15C. By the mere fact that we have considered a thing in joy or in sadness, of which it is not the efficient cause, we can love it or hate it.

This is where sympathy and antipathy come from, this "associative" love or hate: I find so-and-so likeable because I find in him something I once considered joyful. There's nothing mysterious about these feelings, no "occult causes", as Spinoza puts it, but the law of random encounters.

Proposition XVI goes on to explain the mechanism of transference, another point on which Spinozism's psychology could be compared to Freud's! However, this transference most often uses secondary traits. I like X because he looks like Y. But the property P that is common to X and Y (their resemblance) has nothing to do with why I like X. This mechanism, which makes our feelings seem irrational, finds its reason in the central role played by the imagination. Why does Swann fall in love with the demi-mondaine Odette? She "wasn't his type", but she evokes a Botticelli painting for him, and he finds her beautiful. Proust's entire *La Recherche is* based on associations of this kind.

Proposition XVII introduces the explanation of a third state between joy and sadness, which Spinoza calls "fluctuations of the Soul" (in Latin, *fluctuatio animi*). In fact, *fluctuatio animi is* not an exceptional state, but the most common. Subjected as we are to incessant movement, we can only move ceaselessly from the positive pole to the negative pole and vice versa, from an increase in the power to act to a decrease in the power to act, and vice versa. This is because the two feelings coexist in an unstable equilibrium, where even the slightest change can tip one way or the other.

But how is it possible for the same object to have contradictory effects? Spinoza's explanation is still strictly "materialist" (if we can still use the term):

E3P17S. The human body is in fact made up of a very large number of individuals of different natures, and as a result, it can be affected by a single body in many different ways.

To understand what Spinoza is saying, think of the effects of the sun, for example, which are both beneficial and dangerous for the human body.

We are constantly subjected to the contradiction of feelings. It's impossible to find in Spinoza the ideal ataraxia of the Epicureans or the Stoics, because man is not an empire within an empire, and so he is necessarily and necessarily affected by feelings that most often contradict each other. Peace of mind is but a fragile balance between opposing forces.

Proposition XVIII introduces fear and hope as sadness and love related to things past or future. We note that hope is an inconstant joy. Far from being a desirable feeling, it is a fragile one that can easily turn into its opposite. Fear and hope most often place the mind in a state of fluctuation: when I hope, I fear at the same time that my hopes will be disappointed. In Spinozist ethics, neither hope nor despair have any desirable place (here again, Spinoza is as far removed from the theological virtue of hope as he is from the black pessimism of the misanthropes). In fact, all this analysis is easy to understand if we don't forget that the object of feeling is not the thing itself, but the idea of how the thing affects the human body (imagination).

Starting with primary feelings, we can see how Spinoza introduces all the other feelings by composition, or as in a kind of combinatory of passions. The mind is affected not only by the image of an external object, but also by the various ways in which it can imagine that object. I can imagine something that is not present, but whose presence in the future is supposed to make me happy, or sad.

Propositions XIX and XX complete these analyses: the desire for the beloved object leads to the desire for the beloved object to persevere in itself. We could speak of a "*conatus* of transference": my effort to persevere in my being leads me to imagine with joy the effort of another to persevere in his being. P20 seems simply to complete P19 by envisaging hatred through transference. But it goes further by highlighting the formation of a complex (joy arising from the imagination of the destruction of a hated object) that will be a kind of prototype for all the complexes whose formation is analyzed in the following propositions, since the two feelings, joy and hatred, are here completely intertwined (and not simply opposed, as when one is caught between two contrary feelings).

Following on from what is outlined in proposition XIX, the things to which the formations of complex feelings are related are no longer neutral things on which the imagination has accidentally fixed itself. They are things that we can imagine are themselves prey to affects. Our whole social, or rather interpersonal, life is subject to these relationships. Now we're talking about feelings that involve the subject's relations to others, and which have the feelings of others as their object. We could call these feelings "second-order feelings": the mind is not affected by the imagination of a thing, but by the imagination of the feelings of another individual, or by the imagination of the imagination of a thing.

The mimicry of feelings

This is a qualitative step that will take the mind completely into the labyrinth of interpersonal relations. Transference implies a transfer of feelings opposite to that analyzed in proposition XIX.

- *He who imagines what he loves as affected by Joy or Sadness will also be affected by Joy or Sadness* (E3P21).

- He who imagines the one he hates to be sad will be joyful, and vice versa. (E3P23)

- Therefore we will love whoever makes the one we love happy, and hate whoever makes the one we love sad (E3P22).

- We will hate the one who makes joyful the one we hate... (E3P24)

We could discuss Spinoza's positions as set out in Proposition XXII: doesn't the jealous person hate the person who makes his beloved happy? We'll come back to jealousy later. There is here an "affective contagion" of love (like a contagion of hate). We could also speak of a propagation of feelings: the person whose idea is a source of joy for the beloved becomes, in turn, the beloved. It's a bit like the principle that "my friend's friend is my friend".

What emerges from this series of propositions is a veritable "ontology of the social". Not only has Spinoza moved from considering things in general to people, but above all, individuals are not seen as external to one another, like isolated cells, but as originally linked to one another by ties, interpersonal connections. Thus, the true basis of the social bond is to be found not in the calculations of reason, but in the spontaneous concatenation of passions subject only to the rules of the imagination (a concatenation that can also turn into an outburst). In this way, we become involved in the supposed (imagined) feelings of the thing we love. Here again, experience is more than enough to confirm the propositions Spinoza produces by demonstration.

The imaginary of the other is involved in the constitution of feeling. This is the theory of affective mimicry set out in Proposition XXVII :

Chapter III: Genesis and Classification of Feelings

E3P27. If we imagine that a thing similar to ourselves, and for which we have not experienced any feeling, is affected by some feeling, we are by that very fact affected by a similar feeling.

Typical feelings of imitation: *pity* (imitating someone else's sadness), *emulation* (imitating someone else's desire). Mental mechanisms seem to form automatically. Thus Corollary I states:

E3P27C1. If we imagine that someone for whom we have no feelings affects something similar to us with Joy, we will be affected with Love for him. If, on the contrary, he affects it with Sadness, we will, on the contrary, be affected with Hatred against him.

All feelings produced in this way lose their "moral" character. Pity and benevolence are feelings produced in the same way and according to the same laws as other feelings. From here, Spinoza develops what appears to be an abstract combinatorial system from which all possible feelings are generated. In this way, we can see how the complexity of feelings grows:

- Primary feeling (free).

- A feeling linked to the idea of something in general.

- Sentiment linked to the idea of an individual capable of feelings.

- Sentiment linked to the idea of the feeling of an individual capable of feelings (dual situation, like the feeling of being loved by the one you love).

- A feeling linked to the idea of the feeling of an individual who is himself linked to the feeling of an individual who is also the object of a feeling for the subject (triangular situation, like that found in jealousy: hatred of another believed to be loved by the being we love).

In this tangle, however, we can easily distinguish two main categories of feelings:

- "Altruistic" feelings that take individuals other than the subject as their object.

- Personal feelings about the subject itself.

But these two types of feelings can be combined. For example:

E3P26S. Pride is therefore the Joy born of a man's having a better opinion of himself than is right.

It's something that happens naturally: as we always strive to imagine of the thing we hate what affects it with sadness, and conversely to imagine of whom we love what affects it with joy, "so we see that it easily happens that a man has of himself [...] a better opinion than he is just" (E3P26S).

Consideration of others' judgments in turn acts as an amplifier:

E3P29. We will also strive to do all that we imagine men look upon with joy; on the contrary, we will be loath to do what we imagine men dislike.

To conclude this section, let's note that the imitation of feelings plays a decisive role in the system of the life of the mind. We find it in commiseration (imitation of sadness) or emulation (imitation of desire). But in affective imitation, we have an imagination "squared", i.e. an uncertainty and inadequacy of ideas squared.

All feelings in which affective mimicry plays a central role (pride, humility) are "egoistic" feelings, since, directly or indirectly, it is the subject who is taken as the main object. The thesis that the constitution of social facts proceeds from these interpersonal affective links, in which mimicry plays the fundamental role, was developed by French sociologist Gabriel Tarde (author of a book entitled *Les Lois de l'imitation*, 1890) and is taken up, with explicit reference to Spinoza, by economist Frédéric Lordon, who published *L'intérêt souverain. Essai d'anthropologie économique spinoziste* (La Découverte Poche, "Sciences humaines et sociales" collection, no. 346, 2014).

Love and hate and what comes next

If we understand the mechanisms by which feelings are produced, we now need to understand how they combine and organize themselves from a dynamic point of view. They can either reinforce or contradict each other, leading to fluctuations in the soul, for example in Proposition XXXI:

- A loves B and A loves C and B loves C: the effect will be to reinforce A's love for B.

- A loves B and A loves C and B hates C: we'll have a "flutter in the soul", since A is driven by two opposing feelings: love for C and the mimetic hatred that his love for B should provoke.

What explains these two possibilities is the operation of a universal identification process. What's true of a loved one is ultimately true of anyone in general. This is why we find the same processes in ambition as in love. Ambition (see the scolie of this proposition) stems from the fact that everyone strives to act in such a way that others will approve of him, but at the same time everyone tends to want to order others according to his own "naturalness": so the ambitious person wants others to act like him (he wants to be their leader), but to become the leader he also has to follow the feelings of those he wants to command.

Proposition XXXII describes envy. One might think that there is no order: we pass from love to ambition and envy, then a little further on to mercy. Spinoza's point is to show that the same property of human nature that makes men merciful also makes them envious and ambitious.

In other words, apparently opposite feelings, which we assign opposite moral judgments (being merciful is generally considered "good" and envious "bad"), are rooted in the same mental process and are easily reversible. Quite often, we hate the person we used to pity, for example if he or she has failed to show gratitude or submission. We are no longer dealing with a classification of feelings between vices and virtues, or between good and bad feelings, but with a "neutral" order, one that follows from the path that leads from causes to effects.

Propositions XXXIII and XXXIV pose the problem of reciprocity in love. If A loves B, then A strives to make B love him. The problem of reciprocity in love is posed here as a passion. This is why God's love, as it will be posed from the end of Part Four onwards, cannot be posed on the model of human love.

Proposition XXXV is devoted to jealousy, a sad passion, or more precisely a fluctuation of the soul since it is hatred of the thing loved.

E3P35S. This Hatred towards the thing loved, joined to Envy, is called Jealousy, which therefore is nothing other than the Floating in the soul born of both Love and Hatred, accompanied by the idea of another whom one envies.

Obviously, this analysis of jealousy is obvious when it comes to sexual possession. But there are other jealousies linked to friendship.

The next proposal deals with prolongation and repetition. This could be seen as an anticipation of Freudian repetition. Neurosis is the non-conscious repetition of the repressed, the repressed usually being a censored desire. The desire to repeat the initial conditions of pleasure also explains how, by accident, our feelings can turn to any object (for example, in psychoanalysis, the explanation of fetishism, so amusingly staged in Luis Buñuel's *The Criminal Life of Archibald de la Cruz*).

The corollary deals with frustration. Frustration in the same way can be caused by the lack of an object accidentally present at the same time as the thing the subject first took pleasure in.

Propositions XXXVII and XXXVIII explain the power of feelings. Spinoza first shows that :

1) Sadness diminishes our power to act.

2) The *conatus* requires an effort in reaction (it is a question of maintaining the being's capacity to persevere in its being).

3) The same reasoning applies *mutatis mutandis to* joy.

So desire is proportional to the intensity of feeling. The power of feelings is not so much a direct power as a power linked to the reactive capacity of the mind and, at the same time, the body (to be compared with the principle of equality of action and reaction in physics).

In the next proposition, he examines what happens when love turns to hate. He applies the "law" of proportionality of proposition XXXVII: hatred of a beloved person is, all other things being equal, stronger than hatred of a person one has never loved. Here again, the demonstrations of the *Ethics* are in line with the experience and constant teaching of those subtle psychologists who are the great novelists.

Propositions XXXIX, XL and XLI link good and evil to joy and sadness.

E3P39S. By good (bonum), I mean here every kind of Joy, and, moreover, everything that leads to joy [...]; by evil every kind of Sadness, and principally that which frustrates a desire.

This follows on from Proposition IX, which showed that we call the thing we desire "good". So before any other consideration, our moral judgements are passionate judgements! That's why everyone "according to his own feeling" judges what is good. Spinoza didn't stop there when he defined sin and merit (cf. part four), but here again moral judgments remain rooted in this soil of feelings. The difference is that good and bad can be defined collectively, since human beings unite in society for their own benefit.

In proposition XL, we define a principle of reciprocity of feelings: I hate who hates me (this is what happens spontaneously) and in the next:

E3P41. If we imagine that we are loved by another, and believe that we have given him no motive for love [...], we will love him in turn.

As I want to be loved by those I love, by imitation, I will strive to love those who love me. This is a reversal of selfish feeling into altruism. This reversal can also occur in the case of hatred, leading to a state of floating in the soul (corollary); in the case where hatred prevails, we'll want to do harm to the person we imagine loves us: this is cruelty.

Here again, we can see how the same complex system of imaginations can produce seemingly opposite feelings. This is one of the reasons for understanding the following propositions.

Instability of affective states and the development of group psychology

Propositions XLII to XLIV deal with the instability of affective states (e.g. the transformation of love into hate and vice versa.) This instability of affective states results from the combination of feelings, which are like physical forms. Thus hatred is increased by reciprocal hatred, or can be extirpated by love. Hatred turned into love produces a greater love than if hatred had not preceded it.

Propositions XLV to XLVII deal with the formation of group psychology. In particular, proposition XLVI deals with the formation of nationalism. Proposition XLV generalizes the mechanisms of projection. I lend to the other the feelings I have myself. We return here to what has already been said in proposition XXVII. My knowledge of others depends partly on a resemblance and partly on my imagination. It is not primarily a rational knowledge. This explains the formation of common opinion and its fundamentally irrational character. This opinion can be generalized to an entire group simply on the basis of an external or accidental resemblance (E3P46). These are the psychic processes that underlie nationalism, chauvinism and racism.

Chapter III: Genesis and Classification of Feelings

This tendency—which can lead to the darkest pessimism—is, however, immediately counterbalanced. There is necessarily some sadness that accompanies the joy of seeing a hated person destroyed or affected by an evil (E3P47). For Spinoza, man is not a wolf to man, contrary to Hobbes' view. There is something in the passions themselves that makes it possible to think of human community and peace.

Propositions XLVIII and XLIX deal with the intensity of interpersonal feelings. The possible combination, in the imagination of objects of feelings of love or hate, leads to a modulation of the power of these feelings. Love is diminished if we imagine that the object loved is not the sole cause of joy (and the same goes for hatred and sadness). The power of a feeling is therefore its ability to monopolize the whole soul. This is the power of alienation.

Proposition XLIX makes this clear. For Spinoza, there is no such thing as a "free thing", since all finite modes exist only as an effect of the laws of nature. A thing that presents itself as "free" is therefore a thing that presents itself as deriving its necessity completely from itself. It is therefore something we divine. In other words, if feeling is most powerful when we imagine a thing as a free cause, it's because it's in this case that we are the most victimized by our imagination, that we are the most alienated.

On the contrary, by representing a thing as necessary, we diminish the feelings to which it is linked. It's not just a matter of moving from imagination to rational knowledge.

It's simply a matter of multiplying the associated objects, as Spinoza showed in proposition XLVIII.

General Characteristics of Sentimental Interactions

The following propositions demonstrate the uncertainty of affective states. We can be affected by accident (E3P50); this is the case in omens and all forms of superstition: a fact accidentally concomitant with an unfortunate event will become a sign of misfortune.

Men can be affected in different ways by the same object (E3P51). This is because man's judgment is highly inconstant, and dominated by imaginary hopes and fears. This is why "we easily conceive that man can often be the author of both his sadness and his joy" (E3P51S). Once again, the freedom we attribute to man is purely illusory, and this illusion is produced precisely by that which enslaves man, i.e. the physics of feelings that toss him to and fro without his being able to control this movement himself.

Consequently, repentance and self-contentment are classified as feelings in which man is, or believes he is, the cause of himself. They are even very vivid and particularly alienating feelings, since they are what make us believe we are free.

Proposition LII contrasts the impression of déjà-vu, banality, with astonishment. How is this still a feeling? Only in that we are still under the domination of the imagination.

Astonishment at novelty stems from insufficient knowledge, or rather inadequate knowledge, and paves the way for other feelings such as fear, dismay and so on. All of the mind's raptures are thus exposed. It should be noted, however, that surprise alone is not considered a feeling.

The illusion of freedom

In proposition LIII, it's the illusion of freedom that's pointed out again. For it is the same illusion of the independence of mind and body that is at issue:

> *E3P53D. Man knows himself only through the affections of his Body and their ideas. Therefore, when Spirit can consider itself, by this very fact it passes, by hypothesis, to a greater perfection, that is, it is affected with joy, and with a joy all the greater because it can imagine itself and its power to act more distinctly.*

Spinoza expounds the principle of affective maximization. We seek to maximize the joy linked to the exaltation of the mind's power to act. "The mind strives to imagine only those things that posit its own power to act" (E3P54). Conversely, the mind is saddened by imagining its own impotence (E3P55). The scolie demonstrates that men are envious by nature. But this nature is reinforced by education, since "parents usually incite their children to virtue by appealing to the spur of honor and envy alone".

Variability of feelings

Propositions LVI and LVII demonstrate the extreme variability of feelings, or rather complexes of feelings. Proposition LVI demonstrates that the life of the mind is spontaneously a life of passions, subject to the action of that which is outside us and which permanently modifies desire. But this reminder now opens the way to clarifying the purpose of the *Ethics*. The aim, says Spinoza in the scolie, is to "determine the impulsive forces of feelings and the power of the mind over them". The general definitions then make it possible to determine "what is, in quality and quantity, the power of the mind to regulate and repress feelings." This marks the transition to what follows, and thus the possibility of reversing the line of passion.

Feelings differ essentially from one individual to another. The feelings of living beings deprived of reason differ fundamentally from the feelings of humans. Spinoza underlines the difference between a horse's lust and a man's lust. But the most important thing is not this difference in feelings, which confines each of us to our own kind. He emphasizes the difference between the fulfillment of the drunkard who suffers his drunkenness and the fulfillment of the philosopher. This difference underlines the fact that the drunkard is caught up in the flow of affective life, and that it's not a matter of judging or deploring. But at the same time, the example of the philosopher shows that man is not condemned to passively endure feelings, but can on the contrary control them, directing them in the direction of reason.

Chapter III: Genesis and Classification of Feelings

Active Feelings: The Possibility of Reversing Affective Subjection

This last part is perhaps the most surprising of the *Ethics*. It posits that we are affected insofar as we are active. This means, first of all, that action and passion are not separate categories, but complementary poles on the same line, with the permanent possibility of a reversal of one into the other.

There is therefore a kind of possible reversal that draws the lines of liberation, a reversal that has been prepared for in the last lines of the scolie of proposition LVII.

Knowledge and "adequate ideas" are sources of joy. Indeed, the mind necessarily considers itself when it has an adequate idea (since when we know something, we also know that we know it, and so on, cf. part II). So, in considering its own power to know, the mind's object is an idea that reinforces its power, because it no longer undergoes but understands, i.e. an idea that makes us joyful.

So desire relates to us also insofar as we understand, in other words, insofar as we are active.

Hence the conclusion of proposition LIX, which commands the whole reversal of the *Ethics*. All the affectations that affect us insofar as we are active lead back to joy and desire. To philosophize is not to renounce joy and desire; on the contrary, it is to give them maximum extension!

The end of the third part is a catalog of affects that formulates this definition synthesizing all that was acquired at the beginning:

Desire is the very essence of man, insofar as it is conceived as determined, by some affection of itself, to do something.

In short, desire is not a lack, "man's misery"; on the contrary, it is the essence of man insofar as he is determined to act, to produce effects. A man without desire is quite simply a dead man.

Chapter IV:
Man's Powerlessness:
The Dynamics of Emotional Life

The preface sets out what will be developed in Part Four. Spinoza begins by defining **man's servitude**:

> *I call man's inability to govern and contain his feelings Servitude. Indeed, the man who is subject to his feelings does not depend on himself, but on fortune, whose power over him is such that he is often forced to do the worst even if he sees the best.*

We are reminded that man does not want what he wants, and wants what he does not want. The questioning of the will as a faculty of the reasonable mind is pursued here. The important expression is obviously that **man does not depend on himself.** Man is not his own master. As we saw in Part III, he is not "an empire within an empire". Here, we note that this non-autonomy of man is stated in the name of the power of fortune (*fortuna*). Fortuna was the Latin goddess who presided over the fortuitous events of human life. It is also a key concept in Machiavelli, the "penetrating Florentine" whom Spinoza read and meditated on (see the "Machiavellian" *Traité politique*).

Here, Spinoza clearly means that we are subject to an external force, without our "will" being able to influence the course of our own actions. "Even when he sees the best", man is nevertheless led to "do the worst". We return to the themes set out in the previous parts, but this time from the point of view of a man subjected to forces beyond his control, from a subjective point of view—whereas Part III was more a typology of feelings and a statement of their laws as analogous to physical laws.

This brings us back to two classic questions: the will to evil and the "weakness of the will", or the problem of *acrasia* (*akrateia* or powerlessness to govern oneself).

For Plato, "No one is wilfully wicked". In other words, if I know good, I do it, and if I do evil, it's only out of ignorance. This proposition is not the mark of incurable angelism, but is based on a rather precise idea of what it is to will. To will is to try to obtain, and what I try to obtain is what I judge to be the best for me to obtain. In other words, the man who does evil does so because he judges it to be good (at least for him) and he judges that seeking the good for oneself, even at the expense of others, is the first truth to follow in the conduct of one's affairs. How can I persuade him to renounce evil without showing him that good for himself at the expense of others is evil, and that true good for himself is inseparable from good for others. It would seem that, whichever way you look at the problem, you can't separate the will from judgments, and thus goodness or badness from truth or error. To which Aristotle replies that "wickedness is something to which we consent" and that, consequently, "it is up to us to be honest or naughty" (*Nicomachean Ethics*[10], Book III, 1113b). Man is the cause of his actions, and ignorance may be punishable, Aristotle maintains.

The second problem is weakness of will, or "incontinent action". Aristotle defines incontinent action as follows: "Some people, when they have deliberated, do not adhere to the conclusions of their deliberation because of their affections, while others, because they have not deliberated, allow themselves to be led by their affections" (EN, 1150b). But no one can use their affections to justify their incontinence. Indeed, again applying the principle that virtue is a disposition acquired by habit, Aristotle argues that those who "have sensed and foreseen the affection" and "have put themselves on the alert beforehand and placed their reasoning on the alert", these "do not allow themselves to be overcome by affection, whether it be pleasant or painful" (*Ibid.*).

---

10. Quoted here in the translation by Richard Bodéüs, GF/Flammarion, 2004. (The *Nicomachean Ethics* is subsequently abbreviated to EN.)

Spinoza settles this old argument by showing the inconsistency of the will of a man subjected (enslaved) to feelings. He admits that we can see clearly while acting badly, but refuses to consider that man is the cause of his actions. We are not always, far from it, the cause of our actions, and we are, more often than not, powerless, tossed about by the passions that agitate us.

Human powerlessness, however, is not absolute. If it were, man's powerlessness would simply disappear! The aim of Part IV is therefore to explain man's state of servitude by its cause, and to determine "what is good and bad in feelings."

These two objectives thus define a **scientific** ambition (to explain effects from causes) and a **therapeutic** ambition: the aim is not to suppress feelings, but to govern and reduce them.

In other words, Part Four is not content, as its title would suggest, to deal with "the servitude of man or the forces of feeling". It defines the possibility of man's liberation at the very level of his servitude.

Now, to find out how man can begin to liberate himself in a life even dominated by feelings, we have to ask what is "good and bad in feelings". This is a change of viewpoint that may not seem very obvious, since in the third part Spinoza had, on the contrary, endeavored to study feelings "as if they were lines, surfaces and solids", and had thus ruled out any value judgments; the point was, in fact, to take things as they are necessarily determined in the idea of God. From the outset, this point of view ruled out any possibility of a discrepancy between what is and what is good, between the descriptive and normative points of view. If, on the other hand, we look at things from the point of view of the human condition, we now have to make reasoned **assessments.** The botanist studies plants in themselves, while the physician is interested in their virtues or their dangers.

The preface to Part IV must therefore first address the area of validity of the notions of good and bad, or perfect and imperfect. For Spinoza, this means adopting a **genealogical** point of view: seeking to understand how men came to think in terms of good and bad, or perfect and imperfect.

In the third part, we noted a kind of contradiction on the subject of perfection. In the second part, Spinoza writes:

D6. By reality and by perfection, I mean the same thing.

Now, in Part III, Spinoza defines feelings as the passage from a certain level of perfection to another level of perfection. (Cf. Definitions of Joy and Sadness.) This is why, in Part IV, Spinoza has to take up the definition of perfection again, showing that he is not contradicting himself. Spinoza maintains that perfection and imperfection are merely **modes of thinking**, not positive characteristics of things in themselves. The arguments in favor of this thesis are as follows:

1° The common idea of perfection or imperfection is linked to that of good or bad execution of a design. These ideas are thus born in the particular terrain of human

Chapter IV: Man's Powerlessness: The Dynamics of Emotional Life

production of artificial objects, executed with a certain end in view, what the Greeks called *poièsis*. The example of the house, used by Spinoza, is obviously taken from Aristotle, without any explicit quotation. If the finished object conforms to the plan (or the statue closely resembles the model), it's easy to judge its perfection. But even if we don't know what the plan is, we've got into the habit of judging everything in relation to a plan we imagine. Note that Spinoza does not say that things are perfect or imperfect, but only that they will be "said" to be so. This emphasizes the nominal character of these appellations (or "vocables"), which do not refer to true knowledge.

2° It is the generalization of these notions to the whole of nature that is the cause of our ideas of the perfect and the imperfect as absolutes. We find here again the **projective** mechanism that Spinoza has already demonstrated at length in Part One. It is absurd to say that nature produces imperfect things: to do so is to fall into the finalist illusions denounced in the appendix to Part I, which represent nature as guided by a predetermined goal fixed by a transcendent force, a force existing prior to its decrees. Hence the repetition here of the thesis that :

> *What we call the final cause is nothing but human desire, insofar as it is considered the primordial principle or cause of a thing.*

Ignorance of true causes leads people to imagine all natural processes in terms of their own desires. This leads them to ignore the difference between the products of nature and the results of their own actions, and thus to speak in abusive language of the perfection or imperfection of nature. Strictly speaking, we spontaneously take our desires for realities!

3° Perfect and imperfect are notions born of "the comparison of individuals of the same species". These notions result from our mind's inability to form itself to the idea of a large number of singular individuals, and thus from "our custom of reducing all the individuals of Nature to a single most general genus". What we call perfect or imperfect is in fact a certain way of affecting our minds.

Spinoza clarifies his position:

> *As far as good and bad are concerned, they also reveal nothing positive in things, at least when considered in themselves, and are merely modes of thinking, i.e. notions we form because we compare things with each other. Indeed, one and the same thing can be, at the same time, good and bad, and also indifferent.*

In other words, the ideas of perfection and imperfection are the result of man's situation, subject to his feelings and incapable of adequately thinking through the necessity of his own actions. The only correct way of thinking about perfection and imperfection is that defined in Part II (cf. end of preface). If "nothing belongs to the nature of a thing, except

Chapter IV: Man's Powerlessness: The Dynamics of Emotional Life

that which follows from the necessity of the nature of an efficient cause", then it is quite inadequate to speak in these terms. However, the subjective way is unavoidable as soon as we talk about feelings.

Definitions

We start by defining **good** and **bad** (D1 and D2).

> *D1. By good, I mean what we know with certainty will be useful to us.*

It seems to be a **utilitarian** definition. Happiness is the maximization of utility, say modern utilitarians. However, this idea of a relationship between the good and the useful can be found throughout ancient philosophy. This is true of Epicurus, of course, but also of Cicero and even Aristotle. Basically, what is good is that which contributes to happiness, and what is sovereignly good is that which contributes to the sovereign good, which is in fact what orders all human actions. So, as Aristotle puts it: "What is the good that stands at the top of all those that are executable? On one name, in short, the great majority agree: it is happiness, indeed, say the masses and people of note" (EN, 1095a).

But Aristotle adds that this is a rather formal definition, since no one agrees on the very nature of happiness. Aristotle's ethical doctrine is "eudemonism". But for Aristotle, the pursuit of happiness has a very precise meaning: "Happiness is a certain activity of the soul expressing final virtue" (EN, 1102a).

This Aristotelian definition can characterize a wide range of doctrines. It is accepted that man should seek to be happy, but being happy is only possible if we act guided by virtue. There's a kind of circular definition of virtue and happiness, since we now need to know what virtue consists in.

In Thomas Hobbes (*Leviathan*, ch. VI), we find this definition, not far removed from Spinoza's: "But the object, whatever it may be, of a man's appetite or desire, is what for his part he calls good; and he calls evil the object of his hatred or aversion."

As with Spinoza, Good and Evil are subjective judgments, born of the human imagination, which is why we prefer to speak of **good**, which is a relative value, rather than *goodness*. The morality of Spinoza and Hobbes can obviously be contrasted with the morality of Kant. The idea that the value of an act or a thing can be linked to its usefulness to man is one that Kant rejects. He rejects the idea that morality can be founded on empirical principles such as the principle of happiness. He adds (*Foundations of the Metaphysics of Morals*, second section): "However, the principle of personal happiness is the most reprehensible, not only because it is false, and because experience contradicts the supposition that well-being is always regulated by 'doing well'; not even only because it does not contribute in the least to founding morality, for it is quite another thing to make a man happy than to make him good, to make him prudent and perceptive for his own interest than to make him virtuous ; but because it presupposes motives under morality that ruin it and undermine any sublimity; indeed, they include in the same class the motives that impel to virtue and those that impel to vice; they only teach us to calculate better. "

Indeed, we might ask whether the Spinozist definition of the **good does** not include both the motives of vice and those of virtue, thus ruining all morality and ethics. If *good* and *bad* are merely subjective characterizations, how can anyone claim that his conception of the *good* is valid for everyone?

Spinoza would refute the Kantian objection—if Spinoza can be made to polemicize *post mortem* against Kant—with two arguments:

1) Just as objective knowledge of human nature is possible, so it follows that we can objectively define what is good for man. A man submissive to his passions is unaware of his true good (the drunkard sees it in drunkenness). But if all men agree in nature, there is something good for all men and something bad for all.

2) The opposition of prudence and virtue is a pure abstraction. How could the individual be encouraged to practice virtue if he didn't find in it, in some way, a full realization of himself?

Spinoza's definition of the good thus places us at the center of a number of philosophical controversies. It confirms the constant repetition of essential themes in Spinoza's philosophy.

1) Freedom as free will is an illusion.

2) There is no transcendent "reign of ends" to serve as a standard, no plan of nature whose designs we should follow. The end is only appetite (or desire).

3)It is only through knowledge of common human nature that we can define morality and politics.

From the definition of good and bad we move on to that of contingent (D3) and possible (D4) singular things. These definitions seem to come here a little like a "hair on the soup". They would have been better placed in Part I. Spinoza clarifies the difference between contingent singular things and possible singular things. A man is a contingent singular thing, since his existence (or non-existence) is not posited in his essence. A singular thing is said to be possible when we refer to the causes of its production. The category of the possible obviously raises questions:

- We know that the contingent is contingent only for us: a thing is said to be contingent when "turning our attention" to its essence alone, **we don't find** what makes it necessary. But in God, of course, the thing is always necessary.

- Possible is also a category "for us", not "in itself". A thing is possible when, considering its causes, we see nothing that necessarily determines it to be produced.

The opposition between these two categories is only very relative (in general, there is no distinction to be made between

Chapter IV: Man's Powerlessness: The Dynamics of Emotional Life

contingent and possible, cf. E1P33S). It only becomes interesting when we try to think about action.

The introduction of "possible" could be interpreted as a shift in thinking, designed to loosen the iron corset of natural necessity that has been expounded in parts I and II, but also III. In other words, the possible would introduce play and the possibility of choice for man. But this is the wrong way to put the question. Limited free will is no more conceivable than free will in general. From the point of view of reality in general, if I consider something to be possible, and I act in order to realize this possibility, all these facts are linked together according to the strictest causal determinism. But from the point of view of the subject of action, the same is not true: as a "natural thing", the individual seeks to maximize his power, and it is from this point of view that he considers the possible. And, of course, it makes all the difference whether the individual envisages possible things with adequate or inadequate ideas.

The following definitions are summaries of what we learned in Part Three (D5, D6 and D7). Contrary feelings (D5) are contrary only insofar as they pull man in opposite directions. They are contrary by accident, but not in themselves or by essence. Indeed, feelings of the same kind can pull man in two opposite directions (as in the case of gluttony and avarice, which are two kinds of love, love of money and love of food). Here we return to the theses of the third part, which show that feelings are never good or bad in themselves; they must escape value judgments and be studied only in terms of their action. We had also seen that two sentiments that seem contrary in the eyes of ordinary morality, such as mercy on the one hand and envy and ambition on the other, derive from the same property of human nature. (E3P32).

Definition VIII has a central place. Firstly, because the definition of *virtue* is the central question of all ethical philosophy. Secondly, because Spinoza identifies virtue with *power*. It is defined as man's nature "insofar as he has the power to do certain things that can be understood by the laws of his nature alone". Virtue or (*seu*) puissance, then, are defined as another way of talking about effort or *conatus*, i.e. the original impulse that determines the individual to act. The use of the terms power and virtue also reveals the meaning of Spinoza's ethics. What is **virtual** or **potential** is what must be actualized. The liberation of man, the object of ethics (cf. part V), is therefore the development of power, or the fulfillment of all the potentialities contained in this original movement, which are thwarted as long as man is in the bondage of feelings.

The axiom states that power is never absolute. Given a thing, there is always a more powerful thing that can destroy the first.

Chapter IV: Man's Powerlessness: The Dynamics of Emotional Life

The Human Condition is Enslavement to the Passions

The starting point is the power of confused or false ideas, and of imagination in general. Proposition I is quite astonishing:

E4P1. Nothing positive about a false idea is suppressed by the presence of the true, as true.

With this proposition, Spinoza tells us that imaginary representations have a power of their own; they **resist** the manifestation of truth. This is something we know well from madness: in illness, man prefers his own delusion to the manifestation of truth. False ideas are false only insofar as no knowledge corresponds to them, but as psychological phenomena they are necessary, like all other ideas, they are "in God", and therein lies their own efficacy. The example of the sun perceived two hundred feet away illustrates Spinoza's point. If I "see" the sun at two hundred feet, it's a false idea, but this false idea envelops our body's affection for the sun. This idea is false because it is inadequate, but its inadequacy comes only from our ignorance of the causes that make us imagine the Sun as if it were two hundred feet away. But even if we have learned the cause of this appearance, the reality of the bodily affection at the root of the imagination does not disappear overnight. So knowledge of causes is not enough in itself. Thus "when the sun's rays fall on the surface of water and strike our sight by reflection, we imagine it as if it were in the water, though we know very well where it really is" (E4P1S).

Because the mind's feelings have their own power, rational knowledge is not enough to make man wise. He must attack the power of his feelings, "governing" and "reducing" them, as Spinoza puts it.

Man's powerlessness in nature

The following propositions show man's powerlessness in nature (P2, P3 and P4). E4P2 follows logically from the propositions set out, for example, in the preface to the previous part: man is not an empire within an empire. But it is more precise.

E4P2. We are passive insofar as we are a part of Nature that can be conceived by itself, without the other parts.

Man cannot conceive of himself, i.e. he has no real autonomy: this is obvious, since he cannot be by himself (otherwise he would be God!). As an individual, it can only live with other individuals (in society) and in relation to the other components of nature. Spinoza's theory of the subject's autonomy is therefore non-existent. Or rather, the autonomous subject will never be more than a partially autonomous subject, at the end of a long process of liberation, and which, despite everything, will continue to suffer as a "part of Nature" and "cannot conceive of itself without the other parts".

The following proposition reinforces this idea. Man cannot become superman. His life will always be limited in time and space by the "power of external causes".

E4P3. The force by which man perseveres in existence is limited, and is infinitely surpassed by the power of external causes.

The power of external causes follows logically from the aforementioned axiom. Man cannot fail to be a being of nature, he cannot himself create a "second nature", he cannot escape the order of causes. This, too, is what Proposition IV states:

E4P4. It is impossible for man not to be a part of Nature, and to avoid undergoing changes other than those that can be understood by his nature alone and of which he is the adequate cause.

Man is a submissive. His power to act is limited, since he may experience changes for which he is not the adequate cause. The study of man's nature alone does not allow us to say what he can do, and what he can feel, and what he can know. Hence the unambiguous conclusion, in the corollary to this proposition:

E4P4C. It follows that man is necessarily always subject to the passions, that he follows the common order of Nature and obeys it, and that he adapts to it as much as the nature of things requires.

Man's powerlessness in the order of nature is therefore an **essential** powerlessness. If we adhere to the current interpretation of Descartes' formula of man as "master and possessor of nature" (*Discourse on Method,* Part VI), Spinoza is at the opposite end of the spectrum. Wisdom can only consist in the ability to understand this order, and not in the claim to escape or dominate it (cf. axiom). This idea of man's powerlessness can be seen as a trace of the Greek idea that subjects man to the order of the universe and condemns human pretensions to escape this order, condemning excess, which the Greeks considered to be the only true sin—remember that "Know thyself" means first and foremost: "Know thy own measure. We can also see in this a foreshadowing of certain currents of modern thought, which condemn the folly of man's claim to dominate nature: Man thinks he can escape the laws of nature in his techno-scientific activity, but "nature retaliates", we say in the superstitious language of anthropomorphism. Let's just say that its power is always infinitely superior to man's.

All in all, we must emphasize that Spinoza sees the theme of man's powerlessness and servitude as finitude opposed to infinite substance. As a determined being, man is limited by the power of other beings.

191

Passions as powers alien to the subject: thinking about alienation

The following propositions define passions as alien powers (P5, P6 and P7). Here we can conceive of passion as **alienation**.

Proposition V can be understood as follows: passions cannot be explained by our essence alone, as the preceding propositions have shown. Therefore, the power of a passion cannot be defined by our own power to persevere (otherwise the passion would be explained solely by our *conatus*, and therefore it would be explained by our essence alone).

What is proper to passion, then, is the external cause, and the power of passion thus appears as the power of the external cause. Feelings, which develop within us, appear as foreign forces. We no longer belong to ourselves. We are dominated by external powers that possess us. This is confirmed by Proposition VI:

> *E4P6. The force of a passion, or feeling, can override all other actions of man, in other words its power, so that the feeling remains stubbornly attached to man.*

Here we find a theme that is widespread in philosophy. A theme that the later tradition of German philosophy would name *Entfremdung, i.e.* "**alienation**", becoming a stranger to oneself. It's a theme that takes on a central significance in Hegel and Marx.

Kant compares the passions to a **disease that** refuses all medication, or to a bewitchment that refuses even amendment. If, for Kant, emotions are part of the normal life of a reasonable being like man, passions are aberrations. We can immediately see how this view differs from that of Spinoza, for whom the passions are not aberrations, but part of man's normal life.

Marx sees alienation as the transformation of man's personal power into alien power. This theme is found in the *Manuscripts of 1844,* but also in another form in mature works such as *Capital.* The *Manuscripts* describe the alienation of the worker.

> *"Alienation appears not only in the fact that my means of existence is that of another, that what is my desire is in the inaccessible possession of another, but also in the fact that everything is itself other than itself, that my activity is other, and finally—and this also applies to the capitalist—hat it is inhuman power that reigns universally."*

The theme of alienation appears again in Marx more explicitly in two forms:

-It appears as an inversion of reality. Social relationships between individuals appear as things. Things and money are "personified" and appear to have a life of their own (money miraculously produces money).

-In the labor process, man produces the machine, but in the capitalist relationship, the worker is enslaved to the

Chapter IV: Man's Powerlessness: The Dynamics of Emotional Life

machine. The product of man's labor thus appears to him as a foreign power, his enemy.

We could also evoke Freud's theme of alienation. In all cases, there is a common thread: the transformation of an affection of the human spirit into a power foreign to the spirit, the doubling of man in the vital process.

Passionate dynamics

Proposition VII emphasizes that only a feeling can oppose a feeling. So we can already guess that it is only in the government of passions that wisdom will reside, or at least that wisdom can only be possible through the government of passions (and not their suppression).

In Proposition VIII, Spinoza is interested in what we call good or bad, in other words, what we designate by this name, and not in the essence of good and bad considered in themselves, since these designations have no intrinsic value. Spinoza is therefore going to attack our system of spontaneous values. This spontaneous knowledge of good and bad (or right and wrong), since it is not based on reason (knowledge of the second and third kinds), is in reality the simple awareness of a feeling of joy or sadness.

E4P8. The knowledge of good and bad is nothing more than a feeling of joy or sadness, as long as we are aware of it.

Natural man is an "amoral" being, and behind all virtuous behavior, Spinoza invites us to look for motivations in terms of the individual's power or utility. From this point of view, Spinoza's *Ethics* begins with a "philosophy of suspicion" that is much closer than one might think to the French moralists (Pascal), and which can be compared, without overstating the case, to that of Nietzsche. In *The Genealogy of Morals*, Nietzsche proposes to question "the value of values". For Nietzsche, moral values are elements of a vital strategy. Morality can only be justified in relation to vital instinct. Like Spinoza, Nietzsche also subjects free will to criticism.

In Proposition XXIV, Spinoza gives a definition of virtue that could certainly be accepted by Nietzsche, at least in part. The difference—and it's not a small one—lies in the phrase "under the guidance of reason".

E4P24. To act by virtue absolutely is nothing other than to act, to live, to preserve one's being (these three words mean the same thing) under the guidance of Reason, according to the principle that we must seek the usefulness that is proper to us.

To conclude on this point, we should note that good and bad are therefore subjective notions, linked to the finalistic awareness I have of my appetites, when I look for what is useful to me.

Propositions IX to XIII set out the principles of a **mechanics of the passions**. Indeed, as sentiments are classified in

Chapter IV: Man's Powerlessness: The Dynamics of Emotional Life

Part III in terms of power, we move here to their dynamic combination, which is indeed a mechanics of the passions. Propositions IX to XIII study the causes of variation in the intensity of the passions. The gradation of intensity varies from plus to minus according to several parameters:

1)   Imagining the cause as actual or not: for example, the lover's heart beats faster if he knows his beloved is in the next room and not five thousand kilometers away (P9).

2)   Imagining the cause as present or not. For example, anger at something in the past is always weaker than anger at something in the present.

3)   Imagining the cause in the near or distant future. The student is less anxious about the exam at the beginning of the year than about the date of the exam (P10).

4) Imagining the cause as necessary, possible or contingent. What is necessary is indeed endowed with certainty, what is possible is foretold, while what is contingent can take place just as well as its opposite. As Jean-Claude Fraisse[11] says to illustrate this point: "We dread death more than illness, and illness more than a tile falling off a roof."

Faced with this system of passions, whose quantitative laws Spinoza has just exposed, reason appears powerless. This is what the following propositions show.

---

11. Fraisse (Jean-Claude), *L'Œuvre de Spinoza*, Libraire philosophique J. Vrin, 1978.

E4P14. True knowledge of good and bad cannot, as true, counteract any feeling; it can only do so insofar as it is considered a feeling.

True knowledge and feelings are incommensurable. They are not of the same order. Spinoza tells us that since feeling is an idea that expresses a force of existence in the body, greater or lesser than before, it has, in itself, nothing positive that could be taken away by the presence of truth. But we have seen, in propositions LVII and LVIII of Part III, that rational knowledge is a source of joy and that therefore we can be affected insofar as we are active. So true knowledge of good and bad can reduce a feeling, insofar as it is the source of a stronger feeling. So there's no getting away from the flow mechanics of emotional life.

Consequently, a desire born of true knowledge can be destroyed, defeated, by the greater force of a passion, says proposition XV. And in particular, says Proposition XVI, rational desires for future things so easily succumb to irrational desires for present things. The drug addict desires to desist from the drug with a view to future health, but succumbs to the desire for his present drug. Proposition XVII confirms that the immediate appetite, for the reasons set out in Proposition X, most often has the upper hand.

From all this it follows that:

P17S. Men are more moved by opinion than by true Reason.

One might think that Spinoza would join the camp of man's contemptors in denouncing the power of sensual appetites. Even if "he who increases his knowledge, increases his pain"—he says, quoting Ecclesiastes—the point is to reject consolatory illusions, to determine precisely what reason can and cannot do in the government of feelings.

Although in Part IV Spinoza does not deal with the power of reason, but only with man's impotence (cf. the scolie of proposition XVII), a liberation appears within this horizon of servitude.

Virtue has a natural foundation

The principle of proper usefulness is the natural foundation of virtue, as set out in propositions XIX to XXII. Proposition XIX states in another form a principle that has already been announced several times:

E4P19. Everyone, according to the laws of his nature, necessarily desires or dislikes what he judges to be good or bad.

Spinoza's propositions can be compared with those of Hobbes. For Hobbes (*Leviathan*, ch. XIV), they form the basis of the "right of nature" (*jus naturalis*), which is "the freedom of each person to use his own power as he wishes for the preservation of his own nature".

We can also quote Rousseau (*Social Contract*, I, chap. II) for whom the first law of human nature is "to take care of his own preservation, his first care is that which he owes to himself, and, as soon as he is of age, he being the sole judge of the proper means to preserve himself becomes thereby his own master."

We could also show the differences between these three authors. But these differences are beyond our immediate scope. It should be noted that the priority given to self-love, which lies at the foundation of the philosophy and ethics of these three theorists of the modern state, can also be founded theologically: the preservation of one's own being is one of man's essential duties according to the theologians, and Kantian morality will also emphasize the importance of the duties we owe to ourselves. The novelty or break with tradition introduced by Spinoza with this principle of proper usefulness should not be overestimated. Its particular value lies in the way it fits into the overall system.

Proposition XX, which completes the previous one, links virtue directly to power, which is the real break with the Christian tradition and the real opposition to the morals of duty. Virtue must be taken in its etymological sense: for the Greeks, *arete* is the quality by which one excels. Latin *virtus* is a direct translation of Greek *arete*, and it is only in a derivative sense that it comes to refer specifically to moral qualities.

So for Spinoza, living well, attaining beatitude and living fully are synonymous, as proposition XXI explains. So *conatus*, effort, is itself virtue, it is the first virtue, and no prior virtue can be conceived (P22).

Spinoza thus establishes the **natural foundations** of morality; in other words, we can only behave well by following Reason, which is nothing other than the understanding's perception of the natural chain of causes. If we are determined to act by inadequate ideas, we cannot be said to act by virtue. Virtue presupposes knowledge. The flip side of the theory of morality as conformity to the order of nature thus appears as an **"intellectualist" conception of ethics**. Here again, we must contrast Kant with Spinoza. For Kant, the order of practical reason and the order of knowledge—pure reason—are two different orders. Spinoza denies that there is a will distinct from the understanding, whereas Kant, like Descartes, clearly separates these two "faculties". Moral philosophy, for Kant, "applied to man, does not make the slightest borrowing from the knowledge of what he is (anthropology); on the contrary, it gives him, insofar as he is a reasonable being, *a priori* laws." This is why Kant attaches less importance to the critique of practical reason than to the critique of pure reason. Indeed: "[...] in moral matters, human reason, even in the most common intelligence, can easily be brought to a high degree of accuracy and perfection."

And Kant adds that this "metaphysics of morals" can therefore be "popular". On the contrary, for Spinoza, the path to beatitude is not within everyone's reach; ethics is not "popular"; on the contrary, it is an "arduous path", as the last lines of the book put it. This opposition between Kant and Spinoza is not, however, a term-by-term opposition, because it is first and foremost the issues that are different. Kant is looking for the principles of morality, while Spinoza is wondering about the path to Wisdom. He who does not act out of virtue is not vicious, but ignorant. Spinoza still has something of Socrates' "no one is wicked voluntarily". If we act according to knowledge, we act well. Whereas Kant, as a good Augustinian Protestant, always keeps original sin in the background. Let's add that the knowledge of which Spinoza speaks is not necessarily the scholarly knowledge of those who have followed the path of formal studies. The only true knowledge is the knowledge of how to live well, the knowledge of man and his feelings, which requires neither a specialist in physics nor a professional mathematician, and so on.

So, as has already been said, Spinoza sums up the entire *Ethics* in a condensed formula:

> *E4P24. To act by virtue absolutely is nothing else in us than to act, live and preserve our being (these three words mean the same thing) under the guidance of Reason, according to the principle that we must seek the useful that is proper to us.*

Proposition XXV teaches us that, whatever the motives for action, whether conscious or unconscious, we act only with a view to preserving our own being. Thus the reconciliation of private and collective interest, as explained in the scolie of proposition XVIII, is not due to a hypothetical altruism, but rather to the consequent application of a point of view of being's striving to persevere in its being.

Is this egoism? No, because the individual has no choice in self-preservation. It is imposed on him by natural laws that he has no power to change.

These ideas, which make self-interest the foundation of human behavior, are in the air of the times, since similar formulas can be found in Thomas Hobbes. The eighteenth century, with its French materialists (d'Holbach) and English economists (Smith), showed that egoism and the pursuit of one's own usefulness were compatible with collective social and moral progress. Helvétius (*De l'esprit*) explains that "interest is the sole judge of probity and wit." He adds: "If the physical universe is subject to the laws of motion, the moral universe is no less subject to those of interest. On earth, interest is the powerful enchanter who changes the form of all objects in the eyes of all creatures."

The formulas of Baron d'Holbach (*Système de la nature ou des lois du monde physique et du monde moral*) are quite similar: "[...] what is man's goal in the sphere that occupies him? It is to preserve himself and make his existence happy. [...] Thus virtue is everything that is truly and constantly useful to beings of the human species living in society; vice is everything that is harmful to them."

However, utility is not related directly to the individual, but to the individual via the human species living in society. We'll come back to this question in a moment.

For Spinoza, it's not a question of flat utilitarianism (calculating pleasures and pains), because the useful thing par excellence is knowledge, and more precisely knowledge of God:

E4P26. All that we strive for according to Reason is nothing other than understanding; and the Spirit, insofar as it makes use of Reason, does not judge anything else to be useful to it, other than that which leads it to understand.

And so:

E4P27. We know with certainty nothing that is good or bad, other than what actually leads to understanding, or what may prevent us from understanding.

What we have here is a veritable **reversal of ends and means**. Knowledge is first presented as a means to an end. Now, in these last propositions, it has become the end itself. This is what fundamentally distinguishes Spinoza from later utilitarians. Utilitarianism aims at action; it is part of a rationality guided by practical goals (well-being, the wealth of nations, progress). In a surprising reversal for Spinoza, utilitarianism finds its consecration in a purely contemplative attitude, which is yet another mark by which Spinozist modernity remains attached to the ancient philosophical or religious tradition.

Thus proposition XXVIII states:

E4P28. The sovereign good of the Spirit is the knowledge of God, and the sovereign virtue of the Spirit is to know God.

To know God is to know nature, all that is. The path to bliss, the path guided by our own usefulness, is therefore to know as many things as possible adequately. But adequate knowledge presupposes that we are able to overcome the prejudices of our spontaneous finalism, which is itself only the result of the fact that we desire what is useful to us. We thus rediscover the old ideal of the supreme good as contemplation, which is that of Plato and Aristotle. This may seem contradictory to previous developments. In fact, as Jean-Claude Fraisse puts it: "It is in the profound identity between reason and *conatus*, that *conatus* of which the affective life nevertheless gives us knowledge through its own sequences, that the only possible possibility of progress in relation to pure passivity will be found."

The contradiction we've mentioned would only be possible if we were to posit the idea of a transcendent reason opposed to irreducible passions, an idea by which we would be reduced to despair. But this is not Spinoza's thesis, which postulates the profound identity of reason and *conatus*.

From Proper Usefulness to Common Usefulness: The Genesis of Sociability

These propositions develop what had been stated in abstract form in the scolie of proposition XVIII. We find the rational principles on which Spinozism's politics is founded.

Propositions XXIX to XXXI set out the principle of sociability in abstract form. Let's summarize the reasoning:

1) Good or bad can only be that which has a certain relationship with us, that which has something in common with our own nature.

2) To the extent that something has something in common with us, it can't be bad.

3) So a thing is good for us insofar as it accords with our nature.

The central point of this demonstration is the idea of **agreement in kind**.

However, Proposition XXXII states:

E4P32. Insofar as men are subject to passions, we cannot say that they agree by nature.

Spinoza justifies this assertion with an argument that sums up his entire philosophy: the nature of a thing is its power, and the passions are man's impotence, so to agree in impotence cannot be to agree in nature. Agreement cannot be made on purely negative criteria: black and white cannot be said to agree on the grounds that they are not red. Hence this conclusion:

> *E4P32S. Things that agree in negation alone, in other words in what they don't have, don't actually agree in anything.*

Apart from the logical value of this proposition, we must immediately grasp what it means in concrete terms: passions are not a source of union, but a source of division between men. This is obvious in the case of passions that lead to exclusive possession: love, wealth or power are the source of incessant conflict. But not only do men differ from one another in their passions, they are also divided within themselves by their own inconstancy.

We need to clarify the process of this division, which Spinoza analyzes with subtlety. The love that two men have for the same woman cannot in itself be a source of hatred. In fact, according to Spinoza, it is an agreement by nature, and "these two men are not importunate to each other insofar as they agree by nature, that is, insofar as they both love the same thing" (E4P34S). If there is hatred between them, it's because one's possession of the beloved object is the other's loss of that same object, and so this is where they differ. This is because the object of love is a finite object. Again, we see how, for Spinoza, love and possession not only do not go hand in hand, but even contradict each other in their effects.

Proposition XXXV seems to offer a solution:

E4P35. Insofar as men live under the guidance of Reason, they always necessarily agree by nature.

By acting according to reason, men do what is good for human nature, and consequently "for every man." This is because to act according to reason is to act according to man's own nature, whereas to suffer is not to be the adequate cause of one's own actions, but to undergo the action of forces external to oneself.

But the scolie clarifies what is meant by this. If men repeat that "man is God for man", practical experience shows that these are just words. For:

Yet it's rare for men to live under the guidance of Reason; but that's the way it is: most of them are jealous of each other and can't stand each other.

It is not that man lives under the guidance of reason, but that he is a "social animal". Spinoza takes the opposite view of Hobbes' thesis that man is a wolf to man. Hence the renewed polemic against theologians and melancholics who depreciate man and praise beasts.

These two propositions, and especially the scolies that follow the last one, reiterate that to follow virtue is to act for the good of all men. We cannot desire the good for ourselves alone if we live under the guidance of reason.

E4P36. The sovereign good of those who practice virtue is common to all, and all can equally find their joy in it.

And so:

E4P37. The good that anyone who practices virtue desires for himself, he will also desire for other men, and all the more as he has a greater knowledge of God.

In the scolie I of Proposition XXXVII, Spinoza defines:

1) **Religion**: "[...] all the desires and actions of which we are the cause insofar as we have the idea of God [...]."

2) **Morality**: "[...] the Desire to do good which derives its origin from the fact that we live under the guidance of Reason [...]."

3) And **Honesty**: "[...] to bind others by the bonds of friendship [...]."

Religion is defined here abstractly enough for the believer to recognize himself in it. But obviously, for Spinoza, it's not about superstitious religions, those that produce anthropomorphic gods, but about knowledge of God or nature.

Spinoza's definition of virtue and of acting under the guidance of reason enables him to settle a number of practical problems (for example, the relationship between man and animals: unlike Descartes, Spinoza admits that animals feel (but *feel* should be understood as "being aware"), but he asserts that man nevertheless has the right to dispose of them as he sees fit: right is simply a question of power, and since man's power is greater than that of animals, he can impose his natural right. What's more, animals don't agree with us in nature, and don't have the same feelings as we do.

Scholia II sets out the foundations of morality, law and politics (found in the *Political Treatise*). It attempts to define the rules of value judgments (praise and blame, merit and fault, just and unjust). But these rules cannot be defined abstractly. They only make sense if we consider man in the state in which he lives in society. Man is a "social animal" (Spinoza would agree with Aristotle here), but he must be considered in two respects: as a natural being, i.e. as an individual, and as socially bound to other men.

This distinction wouldn't make much sense to Aristotle, since man is naturally a "political animal" (a man living alone would either be a God or a monster). But for Spinoza, the individual dimension is just as essential as the social one.

He thus defines the **Law of Nature** as the supreme right, expressed in terms almost identical to those of Hobbes.

P37S2. Each one exists by the sovereign right of Nature, and consequently each one, by the sovereign right of Nature, does what follows from the necessity of his nature; thus, by the sovereign right of Nature, each one judges what is good, what is bad, and thinks of his utility according to his own naturalness.

Chapter IV: Man's Powerlessness: The Dynamics of Emotional Life

But as men cannot all live under the guidance of reason, they must, in order to live together, renounce this natural right (in part) and unite with one another to increase their power. This is precisely what the constitution of the city and political power are all about. This is not an "unnatural" operation (indeed, reason commands nothing that is unnatural), but a logical extension of the need to preserve each individual's own nature. Here again, we might compare this passage with Hobbes' law of natural conservation.

From then on, we can talk about fault and merit. Spinoza derives fault not from man's natural state (in the state of nature, it is inconceivable), but from his civil state.

E4P37S2. Fault is therefore nothing other than disobedience, which for this reason is punishable under state law alone.

Therefore :

E4P37S2. Clearly, then, just and unjust, fault and merit are extrinsic notions, not attributes that explain the nature of the mind.

The role of **the institution** in the practical life of men is thus decisive. The political institution thus appears as the means by which the demands of reason can coexist with the weakness of men who are subject to their passions.

We'll come back to this specific question later.

From Servitude to Freedom

In Part III, feelings were classified according to their mode of production. Now they will be classified according to whether or not they enhance man's power. Thus, anything that disposes the body to be affected in the greatest number of ways and to affect other bodies is useful, since it strengthens the mind's capacity to perceive more things (P38). So is anything that helps maintain the body's physical integrity (P39). Finally, anything that helps establish harmony between people is useful.

As we can see, the *Ethics* presuppose a certain type of relationship with the body. The fact that Spinoza classifies the passions according to their relationship to bodily movements is by no means secondary. Like Epicurus' philosophy, the *Ethics* is a **medicine**. It is also a doctrine that aims to develop social life.

Happy knowledge?

Although **disillusioned**, Spinozist determinism is not pessimistic; it defines what is good, and everything it proposes could be called, to use Nietzsche's expression here, a "**gai savoir**":

> *E4P41. Joy is not directly evil, but good; Sadness, on the contrary, is directly evil.*

This is not to say that all joy is always good. Some joys can have excesses or be provoked by objects that in total lead to the weakening of the individual. But:

Chapter IV: Man's Powerlessness: The Dynamics of Emotional Life

Along with gaiety, Spinoza defends **laughter**. Note that a certain Christian tradition condemns laughter as impious (see the quarrels reported in Umberto Eco's novel *The Name of the Rose*), relying on *Luke's Gospel*: "Woe to you who laugh now, for you will mourn and weep" (Lk 6:25).

But the "sensation of pleasure" (titillation!), which is joy, can also be bad. Like desire and love, it can have excesses, whereas pain, which is sadness, can be good.

Joy—and all its derivative forms—is of fundamental importance in *Ethics*. If man cannot live solely under the guidance of reason, he will fight harmful tendencies with joy. And as long as he lives under the guidance of reason (i.e. is active), he will be affected by joy, as explained in Part III. Conversely, all feelings of the sad type, such as hatred, disesteem, etc., are always bad. Once these principles have been established, it's a question of balance. Thus, titillation (or tickling) can be bad in that, being based on the excitation of certain parts of the body, it "prevents the Body from being able to be affected in a very large number of other ways" (E4P43D), which contradicts the principle defined in proposition XXXVIII. Conversely, pain can be good when it corrects the excesses of tickling.

The reasoned use of pleasures or Spinoza's Epicureanism...

Since titillation is a kind of love, love can have excesses, and since desire is all the greater the greater the affection from which it arises, desire can therefore also have excesses (E4P44). If love, in excess, can be bad, hatred, on the other hand, is never good (bearing in mind that by hatred, Spinoza means hatred towards men). Spinoza's ethics are thus based on a **reasoned use of pleasures,** as clearly set out in the scolie of proposition XLV (corollary II, scolie). Spinoza denounces the "fierce and sad deception" that forbids the taking of pleasures. The parallelism of mind and body shows that driving out melancholy is of the same order as appeasing hunger and thirst. Against asceticism or mortification practices (highly prized in most religions), Spinoza asserts:

> *E4P45C2S. No deity, nor anyone but the envious, takes pleasure in my helplessness and sorrow, and holds for us virtue tears, sobs, fear, etc., which are signs of a helpless soul.*

The wise man must therefore, in contrast to the contemptuous of pleasures, make reasonable use (without excess) of the pleasures of the body. This scolie (along with a few others) shows the futility of interpretations that make the Spinozist *Ethics* a Stoic-type ethics. Disdain for suffering and bodily pleasures, indifference to what does not depend on us—these are essential themes in Stoic philosophy, but they are radically foreign to the Spinozist problematic. On the contrary, Spinozism's attitude to pleasure is much closer to that of the Epicureans, for whom the good of the body is necessary, provided that pleasure is limited to the satisfaction of necessary desires.

Faced with stoicism and Christianity

In the propositions that follow, another Stoic theme is invalidated: the opposition between what depends on us and what does not. We know that, for Spinoza, this opposition is meaningless, since passion, though not dependent on us, is nevertheless within us. It appears as the action of a foreign power on my own power, and my own situation will be determined by this difference in power. For Spinoza, we must not learn to rid ourselves of all passion, which would mean ignoring its objective causes, which "do not depend on us". On the contrary, we must act out of **compensation**. This is the meaning of Proposition XLVI:

> *E4P46. Whoever lives under the guidance of Reason, strives, as much as he can, to compensate by Love—in other words, by Generosity—for the Hatred, Anger, Contempt, etc., of another towards him.*

This proposition is a repetition of the Gospel precept. But for Spinoza, the moral conclusions drawn from the use of reason and the precepts of the Gospel are identical, the

Gospel being merely a popular form through which the moral lessons indispensable to man's social and spiritual life are transmitted (see *Theological-Political Treatise*).

However, Spinozism's ethics seem to clash with Christian ethics on one fundamental point. For the Christian, hope is the theological virtue by which the believer awaits God's grace. For Spinoza:

E4P47. Feelings of Hope and Fear cannot be good by themselves.

They rely on each other, and assume a lack of knowledge and powerlessness. Therefore:

E4P47S. So the more we strive to live under the guidance of Reason, the more we strive to depend less on Hope.

So we have to be "hopeless", i.e. have no hope. The wise man doesn't need hope, because he's fully happy! Similar emphases can be found in wisdoms originating in India. In the *Mahâbhârata, for* example, we read: "The desperate are happy [...]. For hope is the greatest pain, and despair the greatest bliss". Let's understand "despair" here as the absence of hope: there's another reason for refusing hope, and it's the one put forward by Spinoza, which links hope to powerlessness and lack.

Getting rid of what makes us powerless

Since the aim is to remove all feelings that could weaken the power of being, we must rid ourselves, as far as possible, of:

E4P50. Pity in the man who lives under the guidance of Reason is by itself bad and useless.

And therefore:

E4P50C. From this it follows that the man who lives according to the commandment of Reason strives, as far as he can, not to be self-pitying.

Indeed:

E4P50S. He who knows perfectly well that all things follow from the necessity of the divine nature and happen according to the eternal laws and rules of Nature, will certainly find nothing that deserves hatred, mockery or contempt, nor will he have pity on anyone; but, as far as human virtue allows, he will strive to do well as they say, and to be in joy. To this is added that he who is easily pitied and moved by the misfortune or tears of others, often does things of which he later repents; both because we do nothing out of feeling that we know with certainty to be good, and because we are easily deceived by false tears.

It is true, however, that pity enables a person who is not under the guidance of reason to show himself human by being helpful to others: he does out of sentiment what he is incapable of understanding as rationally good, but he is not virtuous in the sense given to this term above.

Likewise, another Christian virtue is condemned along with humility.

E4P53. Humility is not a virtue, in other words it is not born of Reason.

Indeed, it's a sadness born of man's realization of his powerlessness. The same is true of repentance, about which Spinoza even adds that "he who repents what he has done is twice unhappy or powerless" (E4P54). These feelings can only be useful insofar as men can scarcely live under the command of reason. They can then serve as a counterweight to pride, they can compel obedience. The same applies to fear and hope: Spinoza notes that the crowd is terrible because it is without fear... and without reason.

The final propositions in this section deal with pride, self-esteem, glory and vainglory. As with humility, these feelings are contrasted with the goal, which for Spinoza is "inner satisfaction" (E4P52), which can arise from reason. Indeed:

Chapter IV: Man's Powerlessness: The Dynamics of Emotional Life

E4P52D. Inner satisfaction is the joy that comes from seeing oneself and one's power to act. Now, man's true power to act, or his virtue, is Reason itself.

Pride, on the other hand, is both unreasonable and difficult to fight, because it is a joy. While Spinoza believes that glory can be derived from reason (P58), it is more often than not a vain glory that feeds on the "furious desire to overwhelm one another" (E4P58S).

The scolie of proposition LVII recalls the process.

E4P57S. I regard human feelings and their properties in the same way as other natural things. Certainly, human feelings manifest no less the power of Nature—if not of man—and his art, than many other things we admire and take pleasure in considering. But I will continue to note what in feelings can be useful to men or what harms them.

The dual character of Spinozist ethics

It's important to understand the dual nature of Spinozist ethics. On the one hand, it sets out what is in accordance with reason, and on the other, it offers a medicine that does not simply oppose an ideal to a sad reality, but, through a system of compensations, enables us, if not to achieve beatitude—which is only possible for the wise—at least to improve life. In some respects, Spinoza's concept of the passions is akin to Hippocratic medicine. Equilibrium of the humours would correspond to equilibrium of the passions. Beyond this comparison, it is the "Greek" character of this ethic that should be emphasized. Aristotle's ethics are neither excessive nor demeaning; they seek maximum autonomy, but use pleasures with reason, moderation and prudence. At the same time, we cannot fail to be struck by the growing gap between this ethic and religious precepts, as we have seen with regard to pity (or commiseration) and humility. Perhaps, however, we shouldn't stop at this first movement and show that far from cold realism or rational egoism, Spinozism's ethics commit us to a far more demanding morality. Contrasting pity with charity, Jankélévitch writes:

"Commiseration, a precarious and fragile movement of a tenderized heart, becomes unshakeable in the love of charity; the maudlin and superficial sentimentality of the merciful who only loves his suffering neighbor gives way to virile love. Pity is improvisation, sloppy love after the fact or at the last minute. How can we trust this fickle, cyclothymic passion, quickly ignited, quickly consumed, which Spinoza defines tristitia orta ex alterius damno? Spinoza concludes peremptorily: "Commiseratio in homine qui ex ductu rationis vivit per se mala et inutilis est".

Mala et inutilis! This is what no one should reproach charity for: insofar as it is love transfigured into virtue, i.e.

made permanent and chronic, extended to the universality of men and to the totality of the person[12]..."

And indeed, for Spinoza, it is Love that must prevail over feelings that make one sad.

The Place of Reason in the Life of Feelings

Anything we can do under the influence of passion can be done by relying on reason. Spinoza's point in proposition LIX is this: even joy brings no advantage over what we could do by relying on reason. In other words, motives born of passion can be replaced by motives born of reason. So it's better to substitute reason for passion.

Hegel maintains that nothing great has been achieved without passion. Indeed, for Hegel, reason's cunning lies in the fact that it uses the passions to achieve its ends.

"Stones and beams obey gravity, tend downwards and are used to build high walls. In this way, the elements are used in accordance with their nature, and together contribute to the production of a result that limits their action. Passions satisfy themselves in an analogous way; they are realized according

---

12. Jankélévitch (Vladimir), *Traité des vertus* (1949), tome 2, *Les vertus et l'amour*, chap. VI, II, p. 171 (New ed., coll. "Champs Essais", Flammarion, 2011).

*to their natural determination, but they produce the edifice of
human society in which they have given law and order the power
against themselves." (cf. Georg W. F. Hegel, Reason in History).*

For Hegel, the passions are the **active** element in history.
In a way, Hegel reverses Spinoza's proposition. But this
opposition cannot be overstated: both think that the passions
are rationally comprehensible, and Spinoza fully accepts the
political role of the passions.

The following propositions LX, LXI and LXII show how
rational substitution avoids the excesses of desire and takes
into account the interests of the body as a whole.

E4P61. The Desire born of Reason cannot be excessive.

It also means considering everything in its proper order, i.e.
in the sequence of cause and effect. Acting rationally means
acting in the long term, and considering all aspects of each
thing. An immediate pleasure can have harmful consequences
in the long term.

For Spinoza, it's better to act out of reason than out of
fear. This seemingly self-evident proposition gives rise to
a polemic against superstition (a polemic that echoes the
opening paragraphs of the TTP).

*E4P63S. The superstitious, who know how to reproach
vices rather than teach virtues, and who apply themselves*

not to lead men by Reason, but to restrain them by Fear so that they flee evil rather than love virtues, tend to nothing else than to make others as unhappy as themselves; so it is not surprising that more often than not they are unbearable and hateful to men.

The path followed by reason has the advantage of being a direct way to pursue the good. Through the passions, at best, we pursue the good only indirectly.

E4P63C. Through the Desire born of Reason, we pursue good directly and shun evil indirectly.

For Spinoza, ethics must always be approached positively, from the direct search for the good. Evil, on the other hand, does not contain any kind of positivity, since, according to proposition LXIV:

E4P64. Knowledge of evil is inadequate knowledge.

(As we shall see later: knowledge of death is inadequate!) Spinoza rejects morality as an abstract opposition of good and evil. Since he advocates an ethics of power, it is always relative that actions can be evaluated. Thus E4P65 states:

Under the guidance of Reason, we will seek the greater of two goods, and the lesser of two evils.

Similarly, a greater future good is preferable to a lesser present good (E4P66).

Towards Freedom

Propositions LXVII to LXIX show that the free man always sees things from a positive point of view, doesn't think about death, doesn't believe that there is good and evil in themselves (but only relatively). Thus:

E4P67. The free man thinks of nothing less than death, and his wisdom is a meditation not on death but on life.

Spinoza's philosophy is thus totally opposed to Stoicism and Christianity, both of which are meditations on death— although Christ's message can be interpreted differently. The whole "to philosophize is to learn how to die" theme is fundamentally refuted. And since we only die once, it's quite impossible to learn to die. In fact, we cannot have adequate knowledge of evil, since good and evil are notions that we form precisely insofar as we are not free:

E4P68. If men were born free, they would form no concept of good and evil, as long as they were free.

It also implies a refusal of heroism or anything that would make man a "being for death". Courage, certainly, but also prudence.

E4P69. The virtue of the free man is as great in avoiding dangers as in overcoming them.

Spinoza's demanding ethics lead to a true society of free men, of those who are not ignorant. This is set out in propositions LXX and LXXI. The benefits of the ignorant are to be avoided, and only free men can trust each other. But if we take Spinoza's propositions too literally, we are led to an aristocratic vision of social life that is far removed from Spinoza's true thinking. Thus, the free man imposes constraints on himself, even on the ignorant, because "the useful and the honest must be taken into account" (E4P70S). Spinoza also rejects the image of the solitary sage:

Explanation of Proposition LXXIII

Proposition LXXIII closes the fourth part, entitled "De la servitude humaine ou de la force des sentiments". But this fourth part does more than simply describe the strength of feelings, in the classic theme of man's subjection to the passions. It is the dynamic relations between sentiments (or affects) that constitute its proper object and, these relations being known, Spinoza sketches out the possibility of man's liberation on the very basis of affective servitude. This eminently political perspective on liberation is summed up in Proposition LXXIII:

E4P73. The man who is led by Reason is freer in the State where he lives according to the common decree than in solitude where he obeys only himself.

This statement may seem paradoxical for two reasons:

1) How can we be freer when we obey, at least in part, others ("the common decree") than when we obey only ourselves?

2) How can one be freer in the state than in solitude, since in the state, in Spinoza's own words, the individual ceases to judge for himself what is good, and submits to an authority that is not his own?

The stakes of this double questioning are quite clear:

1) While many philosophers, first and foremost Hobbes, assert that law and freedom are antithetical, that acceptance of the common law means renunciation of man's natural freedom, Spinoza argues on the contrary that obedience to the common decree enhances individual freedom and does not restrict it.

2) If proposition LXXIII is true, then the development of human sociability and the strengthening of a well-ordered society

corresponds to our own usefulness. "Man is a political animal", says Aristotle. Spinoza reiterates this proposition, without having to invoke an alleged "natural finality" and so many other highly speculative and ultimately very fragile presuppositions.

To understand this proposition, the best method is first to follow the demonstration. Let's begin by noting that the object of this proposition is "the man who is led by Reason". In fact, it makes little sense to speak of the freedom of someone who is not guided by reason, since, as we shall see, freedom is nothing other than living according to reason, the only way to be the adequate cause of one's own actions.

The demonstration is based on propositions LXIII, LXVI (scolie), XXXVII (proposition and scolie II).

1. Proposition LXIII states, "Who is led by fear and does good to avoid evil, is not led by Reason." Indeed:

1.1. According to Proposition III of Part III, all active feelings, i.e. feelings that are related to reason, are feelings of joy or desire.

1.4. Fear is an "inconstant sadness" (E3P13).

1.5. Therefore he who acts out of fear does not act out of reason.

2. The scolie of proposition LXVI states the difference between the free man and the slave. The latter is he who is driven only by feeling or opinion, and therefore essentially unaware of what he is doing, whereas the former always acts for what he knows to be essential. Conclusion: only he who acts according to reason is free.

3. Now, to act according to reason, for one's own good, is (Proposition XXXVII) to act for the common good: "The good that anyone who practices virtue desires for himself, he will also desire for other men, and all the more as he has a greater knowledge of God."

3.1. We know (P35) that it is men, insofar as they live according to reason, who are the most useful to man, and so he who lives according to reason will strive to help others do the same.

3.2. The scolie of proposition XXXVII also showed that it was rational, if we want to live in concord—that is, if we apply P35—for men to "renounce their right of nature and assure each other reciprocally that they will do nothing that can harm others." But since men are often changeable, to ensure the permanence of concord, it is necessary to use the threat of state power, which forces those who live according to their feelings to take the common good into account.

Let's summarize the demonstration:

To be free is to live according to reason. Reason dictates that we seek to live together with other men. To ensure this common life, the state is necessary. So a man who lives according to reason is freer under common decree than in solitude.

Obviously, to accept Spinoza's reasoning, we need to accept a conception of freedom quite different from this identification of freedom with free will, conceived as an absolute power to choose outside of any other determination. As we know, Spinoza considers this free will to be an illusion: men believe

Chapter IV: Man's Powerlessness: The Dynamics of Emotional Life

themselves to be free because they are unaware of the causes that determine them in one direction rather than another (see the appendix to Part I, or the scolie of Proposition II in Part III, for example). To an illusory freedom of choice, Spinoza opposes freedom as an increase in the power to act, taking the term act in its precise sense: a being is active when it is determined solely by its own usefulness, i.e. when it is the adequate cause of its own actions, which presupposes that it has adequate ideas (E3P1). It is passive when, on the contrary, it is determined by affects.

If we understand freedom as power, Spinozism's politics can be easily deduced: when isolated, individuals act solely on their own decree, and can appear quite free. But in this situation, they are very weak, subject to natural events and the power of other individuals. Conversely, when men unite through the bonds of society, the power of each is combined with the power of the others, so that each benefits from and contributes to this cumulative total power, and each receives the protection of the social body made up of the bodies of the individuals who make up society. We then deduce the virtues that the individual living in society must demonstrate: since life in society is best for him, and only in this way does he increase his freedom, he must act to consolidate this union, and this is why what Spinoza calls "Religion" boils down to the practice of justice and charity, the two virtues that help maintain concord between the members of the city.

Obviously, just as the individual can live not according to reason but according to his feelings, the body politic can degenerate and become unjust and tyrannical. It would then seem that the maxim of proposition LXXIII no longer applies: an individual is freer in solitude than in obedience to a tyrannical common power. But in reality, this is not the case: tyrannical political power is never a common power for long. If the individuals who make up the city see that power is detrimental to their own preservation, that of their children, etc., they are in a sense released from the commitment by which society was created. Tyrannical power is in fact power that returns everyone to the state of nature, forcing them to rely solely on themselves for their own preservation. In this case, there may well be individuals who command others, but strictly speaking there is no longer any common power. Tyranny breeds sedition," says the *Political Treatise*. In other words, the case of a tyrannical state does not contradict the proposition, but confirms it.

Let's conclude with a word. This scolie generalizes: freedom, man's true freedom, is nothing other than fortitude, that is, firmness and generosity. This fortitude concentrates within itself all the most eminently social virtues: "the strong man hates and envies no one, is angry and indignant with no one, despises no one, and shows not the slightest pride." And Spinoza goes on to say: "Hatred must be overcome by love. In other words, the precepts that can be drawn from the Gospels, for example, are those that are perfectly suited to any individual who lives rationally and desires for others what he desires for himself. It's easy to see why Spinoza writes that Christ is the greatest of philosophers: his teaching is exactly that to which every man who wants to live according to reason is led (see MATHERON (Alexandre), *Le Christ et le salut des ignorants chez Spinoza*, Éditions Aubier-Montaigne, 1971—a work that has unfortunately become very difficult to find).

General Conclusions on Part IV

In Part III, Spinoza set up a system for classifying feelings: starting with primary feelings and using a feeling-composition operator, he set out a combinatorial logic of affects or feelings.

Part IV elaborates on the dynamics of passions, in which duration and intensity, balance and compensation play a major role.

But in this system of passions, Spinoza shows how reason can assert its superiority and how it can provide the path to true liberation. Political philosophy, which develops over the course of the propositions, concludes the section: there can be no true freedom for the wise man outside the city.

The appendix is a kind of "survival manual" that summarizes everything we've learned in Part Four.

Chapter V:
Liberation and Bliss

The fifth part of the *Ethics* is dominated by a formula, undoubtedly the most enigmatic of this immense work: "The intellectual love of God". To understand this formula, or at least to try to underline all its difficulties, is to make serious progress in understanding Spinoza's entire doctrine. There is a certain "left-wing Spinozism" that rests on a few pillars that are easy enough to define:

1) Spinoza's God has no real function, and is retained only for tactical reasons.

2) There is a purely materialist reading of Spinoza (for example, Diderot's);

3) Spinoza is the great emancipator, the one who established the necessary separation of religion and state (he is the true inventor of secularism).

None of this is false. We can read Spinoza, at least as far as Part IV of the *Ethics,* by positing the equation God = the totality of things that exist (reality) and therefore the existence of God is a pure tautology. For a formal exposition of this analysis, I refer you to Antonio Crivotti's text published on my Internet pages. If we accept this reading, the whole God thing is nothing but a manoeuvre to escape the (costly) accusation of atheism.

That there is a possible materialist reading (as Diderot and no doubt d'Holbach do too) is absolutely obvious, but it is clearly only a *making sense of*, not an explanation of, Spinoza's work. Incidentally, Hegel points out that Spinoza could just as easily be accused of *acosmism* rather than atheism.

Spinoza's third point is not open to dispute, so explicit is he that he clearly differentiates true religion (justice and charity) from the superstitious religions by which the dominant set out to govern men.

If we accept our point (2) as a simple option from Spinoza and not as the truth of the master's thought, only point (1) remains under discussion: what is the status of God in Spinoza?

We know definition VI from Part I:

> *D6. By God, I mean an absolutely infinite being, i.e. a substance consisting of an infinite number of attributes, each of which expresses an eternal and infinite essence.*

This definition takes shape at the end of an abstract demonstration that leads us to proposition XI of the same part:

E1P11. God, in other words a substance made up of an infinite number of attributes, each of which expresses an eternal and infinite essence, necessarily exists.

An important proposition, followed by three demonstrations and a long scolie. The first demonstration by the absurd is lapidary. It boils down to the idea that it is impossible to conceive of the non-existence of a substance made up of an infinite number of attributes. The other demonstrations remain at a very high level of abstraction. Here, it makes more sense to try and grasp what we're talking about, because the name "God" can obviously mislead those who identify God with a person, or with three persons in one, for example. Since there are no substances or affections in nature, and there can only be one substance, all affections are affections of that substance. Put another way, everything that is is in God, and can only be conceived by God. Spinoza's God, it is sometimes said, is the "great whole", and Spinoza is described as a "pantheist". But this is not exactly the case. There is no trace of "mysticism", God appears as a logical construct: God is simply reality in all its dimensions (or attributes). It is eternal, because its existence does not depend on time. Affections (modes) can be born and disappear, but this birth and disappearance presuppose the eternity of reality: we can only think of becoming on a "background" of eternity. It is infinite for similar reasons. If we think of a finite reality, then implicitly we think of a beyond this finite reality—without which it would be impossible to think of its finitude. When we say that the universe is finite and give its size, we are not referring to the universe as such, but only to the physical universe we can observe and understand today according to the laws of physics we have mastered. But that doesn't mean that reality isn't infinite. In short, for Spinoza—and for us!—it's impossible not to start from the absolute of eternal, infinite reality, which can be explained in an infinite number of attributes.

Having reached this point, and accepted the separation between *deus sive natura* ("God, i.e. nature") as the power that produces realities, and the totality of being (*natura naturans* and *natura naturata*), we can read the *Ethics* without difficulty right up to the beginning of Part V. And that's where the trouble begins! And that's where the trouble begins!

The Power of the Mind in Governing Feelings

The fifth part deals with the power of reason and true freedom, the freedom of the mind, which is called beatitude. The preface leads a polemic against the Stoics and Descartes, who, against all that experience teaches, maintain that the mind can have empire over feelings. The critique of the Cartesian "solution" to the mind-body problem alone would merit a lengthy analysis, as it forms the matrix of any serious refutation of dualism. The preface concludes in a way that is eagerly awaited by readers who have reached this stage of the *Ethics*:

So, since the power of the mind, as I have shown above, is defined by intelligence alone, the remedies for feelings, which everyone actually has experience of, but which I don't think we seem to observe carefully or see distinctly, knowledge of the mind alone will enable us to determine them, and deduce from them everything that concerns its beatitude.

The first propositions continue Part IV, and indicate the means by which the empire of passions can be weakened, if not completely annihilated. As Pierre Macherey puts it, this is a kind of daily mental hygiene. The key to this power we have to govern our feelings is given in Proposition X:

E5P10. As long as we are not dominated by feelings that are contrary to our nature, we have the power to order and chain the affections of the body according to an order that conforms to the understanding.

From this proposition we turn to proposition XIV:

E5P14. The mind can cause all the affections of the body—in other words, the images of things—to be related to the idea of God.

To demonstrate this proposition, Spinoza relies on:
1) "There is no affection of the body of which we cannot form some clear and distinct concept" (E5P4.)

235

2) "Everything that is, is in God, and without God nothing can be or be conceived" (E1P15).

The consequence in Proposition XV is:

E5P15. He who understands himself and his feelings, clearly and distinctly, loves God, and the more he understands himself and his feelings, the more he loves God.

This is obvious if we remember that knowledge is a source of joy. And that if we reduce our knowledge to God, joy now has the idea of God as its cause. And love is joy linked to the idea of an external cause. So to know oneself adequately is to love God. It may seem strange that the human mind should take God as the object of love. But insofar as man understands himself, he understands his place in the chain of causes and effects that constitute natural things, and this produces in him a joy that is born of understanding, i.e. of considering his own power to think. In other words, the love of God and the joy of understanding the nature of things are one and the same. And by the same token, we see that love of God is inseparable from love of man insofar as he exercises the best of himself, i.e. the intellect.

Hence proposition XVI concludes:

E5P16. This love for God must occupy the mind to the highest degree.

The power of the intellect is what enables us to know our affections and therefore to know our feelings adequately and to truly know ourselves, and it leads to love, i.e. here to understanding (taking with oneself) towards whom must "occupy the mind to the highest degree": this is indeed a stable feeling, unlike love linked to the imagination of finite things, which is always unstable and threatened by the soul's waverings. Since we know that hatred must be fought, not with weapons, but with love, it follows that love for God (the consequence of self-knowledge) is the means of opposing all the sad feelings that are the mark of our servitude and powerlessness, i.e. of our ignorance, with a strong feeling that is favourable to our efforts.

Why is this love for God stable? The answer is simple: since God is free of affections, he can't communicate them to us! No one can hate God, and love for God cannot change into hate. And no one can strive to have God love them... But this logical answer must be explained in another way. In the love of God, we are no longer in the affective life, but in a completely different register. The joy that comes from knowledge is not of the same nature as the joyful affects that come from the imagination. If you study volcanoes, you can't hate them, and you can't expect volcanic eruptions to be beneficial! Rational understanding of reality removes all fickle feelings and produces serenity of soul.

Having reached this point, Spinoza sums up by saying: "I have therefore brought together all the remedies for feelings" (scholia of proposition XX) and adds, after a few interesting remarks: "I have thus finished with everything that concerns the present life." What a surprising formula, so full of Christian echoes: to love God in the present life and thus gain eternal life? Is this what Spinoza wants to talk about?

Beyond the Present Life

Indeed, things change dramatically from Proposition XXI onwards. We move from prose to mystical experience," says Pierre Macherey. Let's see how things order themselves and, above all, whether it's really mystical experience we're talking about. Here again, as is often the case with Spinoza, we have a "dialectical" composition of propositions:

1) Imaginations and memories (it's the same thing) are linked to the duration of the body. That's pretty obvious.

2) In God, there is an idea that expresses the essence of this and that human body "under the species of eternity". Essences are eternal: they are not subject to duration.

3) The spirit cannot be absolutely destroyed with the body, but something eternal remains.

So there's something in the life of my mind, in the life of the idea that I am, that goes beyond the present life! The old materialistic atheist resists and wonders what path he has embarked upon, for we are now flirting with something akin to mystical experience, leaving the solid ground of rationalism!

And yet it's absolutely obvious once you've agreed to follow Spinoza to the point we've reached. Let's see why.

The human mind is the idea of the human body. During the life of this body, the mind includes the ideas of the body's affections (the mind imagines and remembers as long as the body has affections, i.e. as long as it is not destroyed). But there is also necessarily, belonging to the mind, something that expresses the essence of the human body, the essence of its ideat, independently of the affections that this body undergoes. This idea that expresses the essence of the body is in God—since everything that is is in God, and without God nothing can be or be conceived. A part of our mind is therefore eternal. This doesn't mean that our spirit is immortal! No, it doesn't. This eternal life of a part of ourselves is not life understood as the indefinite pursuit of our spirit: it has nothing to do with the immortality of the soul. In fact, this eternity of a part of our spirit is not life at all. But there is in our spirit a part that is conceived "under the species of eternity." Spinoza says nothing more here. But we can understand it this way: an adequate idea is one that is thought of in us as it is "in God". In this sense, the mind contains an eternal idea, for we can only think what is, not what is not or what is no longer: as long as I live, I am eternal, and I am still eternal when I am dead, since my eternity, as it were, belongs to me: when I think of myself, then, I am necessarily eternal, since I am life itself, since I am fully: "By eternity, I mean existence itself" (cf. definition VIII of Part I). Or, as Michel

Henry puts it in *Spinoza's Happiness*[13]: "Insofar as we are, we are God."

Note on parallelism

Incidentally, we now understand how misleading the metaphor of parallelism is (cf. *above*). In God, there is an idea of everything, but the extended existence of things (bodies) has nothing in common with that of ideas, which express their essence in the form of eternity. Essences being eternal are compossible, but the extended existence of these essences is not. The essence of the father's body and that of the son's body, in God, are not placed in a temporal order, when we grasp them under the species of eternity (since under the species of eternity there is no before and no after), but it is of the son's essence that he comes after the father in the expanse. Essences in God are all at the same time, but not their existences. This last part of the *Ethics* completely destroys the theory of parallelism, for duration and eternity are not two coextensive orders.

---

13. Henry (Michel), Longneaux (Jean-Michel), *Le bonheur de Spinoza*, coll. "Épimethée", PUF, 2004.

The Third Kind of Knowledge

With the eternal subsistence of a part of ourselves, we have taken a first step towards understanding what Spinoza calls the "intellectual love of God", and consequently towards a richer interpretation of Spinoza's concept of God.

Now we're going to go one step further. And to do so, we need to understand what the third kind of knowledge is.

E5P24. The more we understand singular things, the more we understand God.

Indeed, singular things are only affections of God's attributes... As a consequence, the more we know about reality, the more we know about God (hence our first formulation: God = reality).

The question now is how we know singular things rationally. Here we need to recall what was said in Part Two about kinds of knowledge.

1) We have a spontaneous knowledge of singular things, knowledge of the first kind, knowledge that is truncated and confused, since in reality we only know the images of things, i.e. our mind only perceives the affections with which these things affect our body (an image envelops the idea of the thing and the idea of our body, and is therefore confused).

2) We have adequate knowledge of common notions. All bodies are suitable for something, and so we have an adequate

idea of what they are suitable for. To cut a long story short, we don't know singular things, but we can adequately perceive their relationships (these are the "common notions"), and this is the hallmark of scientific knowledge as we understand it today. If you think about it, the mathematical physics invented by Galileo is a theory of relationships, not a science that tells us what things are in themselves. This second kind of knowledge is called "Reason" in Spinoza.

3) The third kind of knowledge alone is called "Science". But it's an intuitive science. It is knowledge that starts from God and goes to the essence of things.

This third kind of knowledge is a bit mysterious! Macherey finds it enigmatic, and Deleuze says he follows Spinoza up to the second kind, but beyond that, Deleuze is no longer a Spinozist. And indeed, many authors "stall" before the third kind. Yet the question of the intellectual love of God stems from this third kind of knowledge, and just as beatitude stems from the intellectual love of God, if we miss the third kind, we ultimately miss the essential point of the Spinozian enterprise!

E5P25. The supreme effort of the Spirit and its sovereign virtue is to understand things through the third kind of knowledge.

This third kind of knowledge requires a preliminary step: knowledge according to reason, which is knowledge of the great laws of nature. But true science is here, and the more we practice it, the stronger we become, and the stronger we become, the more we desire to know all things according to the third kind.

To get a better grasp of what we're talking about, it's best not to be taken in by the expression "intuitive knowledge", because this third kind is not really intuitive, at least not *prime facie*. Spinoza tells us that this third kind enables us to understand singular things from God. The second kind is the one that allows us, on the basis of common notions, to understand the general (abstract) laws of nature. The third kind, on the other hand, enables us to move from the abstract laws of the divine mode of production to singular realities.

We find the same idea, albeit differently formulated, in a 1679 text by Leibniz entitled "Pensées pour l'instauration d'une physique nouvelle", where we learn that "The most perfect method is to find *a priori* the inner constitution of bodies from the contemplation of God, the Author of things. But it is more difficult and is not for everyone to try." In any case, the third kind is indeed the superior mode of knowledge, since it enables us to chain together in our minds the ideas of things exactly in the order in which these things were produced in God. "From this third kind arises (therefore) the greatest possible satisfaction of the mind" (E5P27).

In this third kind, we know things not insofar as they exist for a certain duration, but "under the species of eternity", i.e. we grasp their eternal essence, and in this kind of knowledge the spirit is engaged itself insofar as it is eternal. Hence this important conclusion:

P30. Our Spirit, insofar as it knows itself and the Body, under the species of eternity, necessarily has knowledge of God, and knows that it is in God and is conceived by God.

To know things under the third genus, then, is to know three things at once:
1) Know yourself, know your body properly.
2) To know God adequately and not by imagination.
3) Know as many singular things as possible.

And all under the species of eternity! That's knowledge that embraces the whole in a single glance, and that's why Spinoza calls it "intuitive".

The Intellectual Love of God

This knowledge, the acme of the intellect's power, is therefore naturally, and for reasons we need not go into again, a source of joy. It is a joy that comes from the intellect and is linked to God as its cause. It is an intellectual love of God.

And Spinoza immediately clarifies:

E5P33. The intellectual love of God, born of the third kind of knowledge, is eternal.

And eternal joy is called bliss. Now, since this beatitude is eternal, it has no beginning and no end, and expresses the supreme perfection of the spirit, a perfection that we do not always perceive during our lifetime, because "while the body lasts" we are subject to feelings that relate to passions.

This is why, at proposition XXXIV, Spinoza slips in this scolie which announces what follows:

E5P34S. If we consider the common opinion of men, we shall see that they are, in truth, aware of the eternity of their mind, but that they confuse it with duration and attribute it to imagination or memory, which they believe to subsist after death.

That's all well and good. Immediately afterwards, however, he puts forward a proposition that leaves the reader stunned:

E5P35. God loves himself with an infinite intellectual love.

And by way of explanation, the demonstration asserts that "God's nature enjoys infinite perfection". There's a real problem here: love is an affect, and as we saw above, a man can't want God to love him, since that would be to want God not to be God: God can't be affected by joy, since to want him to be such would be to want God not to be God (E5P19). Indeed, joy is the passage to a greater perfection. But to want God to pass to a greater perfection would be to suppose that he is not perfect, and therefore that he is not God! So, strictly speaking (see Proposition XVII), God can neither hate nor love anyone.

Doesn't thinking that God can enjoy himself fall right back into the anthropomorphism denounced throughout the *Ethics*? Aren't we back in the realm where thought thinks in images, which is the hallmark of the first kind of knowledge, whereas we're in the third?

This proposition also introduces an ambiguity: until now, we have thought of God's love as the love that man feels for God, and now we see that this love of God is also the love that God feels for himself. Here, then, is a knot of difficulties from which we're going to try to extricate ourselves.

Let's look first at Proposition XXXV:

1) To demonstrate this, Spinoza first refers to the definitions of God from Part I: "Being absolutely infinite". We should therefore discard the metaphorical interpretation of this proposition.

2) But if in French the words "jouir" and "joie" refer to the same root, here we have to make a deviation to Latin. Spinoza calls joy the primary affect of the human spirit, *laetitia*. For the Gaffiot, *laetitia* is "gladness", "overflowing joy". But in the demonstration, Spinoza says: "*Dei natura gaudet infinita perfectione*" ("God's nature enjoys infinite perfection"). *Gaudeo* is to rejoice inwardly, and *gaudium* is satisfaction, contentment. In other words, God's love for Himself is not the same as the love a human can feel for some external cause.

3)   The introduction of *gaudium* is not entirely innocent: it is a term with a strong religious connotation - the believer finds *gaudium* in the love of God, whereas *laetitia is* a secular term. This proposition indicates a leap made by Spinoza in the overall progression of the *Ethics*. And this leap bothers commentators. Macherey comments on propositions XXXIII, XXXIV and XXXVII, and has to treat propositions XXXV and XXXVI separately. The overall economy of the *Ethics* could remain very coherent without these two propositions. But they are there! And they give a whole new twist to the intellectual love of God.

Let's move on to the next proposal:

E5P36. The intellectual love of the Spirit towards God is the very love of God, of which God loves himself, not insofar as it is infinite, but insofar as it can be explained by the essence of the human Spirit considered under the species of eternity; that is, the intellectual Love of the Spirit towards God is a part of the Love of which God loves himself.

If we want to know what the love with which God loves himself is, and which seems so enigmatic, Spinoza offers us a kind of sample here: the intellectual love of the (human) mind towards God is a part of the love with which God loves himself. In other words, the two possible meanings of "God's intellectual love"—the love God has for himself and the love humans have for him—are interwoven: the noun complement of God is a passive subject (the love God has for himself) embedded in an active subject (the love God has for himself).

But obviously, since it is only a part of the whole, the intellectual love of the spirit towards God cannot be identical with the love God feels for himself. God loves himself insofar as he is infinite, i.e. in his very perfection, since what is finite are the affections of the substance, which contain less perfection, i.e. less power, than the substance itself. The human mind is the love with which God intellectually loves himself in a more restricted form, not as infinite (because infinity is really too big to fit in the human mind!) but insofar as it can "be explained by the essence of the human mind".

Mentis amor intellectualis erga Deum est ipse Dei amor quo Deus se ipsum amat, non quatenus infinitus est sed quatenus per essentiam humanæ mentis sub specie æternitatis consideratam explicari potest hoc est mentis erga Deum amor intellectualis pars est infiniti amoris quo Deus se ipsum amat.

Word for word: "The intellectual love of the spirit towards God is itself love of God whose love is itself, not as infinite, but insofar as this one (God) can be explained through the consideration under a species of eternity of the essence of the human spirit." Or again: "God is explained through the human essence considered under a species of eternity." Or: "God is explained through the human essence considered under a species of eternity." This refers to the human spirit considered in its eternal essence (i.e. known under the third kind of knowledge).

Let's follow the P36 demonstration to understand this extraordinarily difficult passage.

This love of the spirit must be related to the actions of the spirit:

1)   We know that the mind is active when it has adequate ideas (E3P3);

2)   We know that there are *feelings of joy and desire that relate to us as we are active* (E3P58);

3)   We also know that *of all the feelings that relate to the mind as it is active, there is not one that does not relate to joy or desire* (E3P59).

In other words, adequate ideas help to increase our power to act, and are therefore joys or desires that positively express our *conatus*. And among the actions of the mind, the knowledge of the human spirit under the species of eternity is of the highest, and therefore provides man with the greatest contentment.

So this love of the human spirit towards God is an action that simultaneously considers the spirit itself and God as its cause, since adequate knowledge is knowledge that encompasses the causes of things (i.e. knowledge in which ideas are linked in the mind according to their mode of production).

So in this intellectual love of the human spirit towards God, God is explained as the cause of the human spirit. Explained means that God expresses Himself in that which explains Him. So God causes the human spirit, causes the human spirit's love for God, and in this love explains Himself. So the love of the human spirit for God is indeed part of the intellectual love by which God loves himself.

The corollary of Proposition XXXVI also holds a new surprise. We have seen that men cannot want God to love them. But here Spinoza explains:

E5P36C. From this it follows that God, insofar as he loves himself, loves men, and consequently that God's love for men and the spirit's intellectual love for God are one and the same thing.

Here are the equivalents we have arrived at:

1)   The wise man who attains the third kind of knowledge intellectually loves God.

2)   God loves himself intellectually.

3)   The intellectual love of the human spirit for God is part of God's love for Himself.

4)   God loves men through men's intellectual love for God, since God's love for Himself envelops the love that men (wise men) have for Him (God loves God, in other words, the human mind intellectually loves God and, consequently, God's love involves the minds of men as its cause).

5) By the same token, man, as part of God who loves God, loves himself.

6) Under the guise of arduous logical reasoning, we have here something that can be found in all the great mystics: the equivalence between love for God and God's love for us. And to make this clear, the scolie continues:

E5P36S. This makes it clear to us what our salvation, in other words, Beatitude or Freedom, consists of: in constant and eternal love for God, in other words, in God's love for mankind.

The resumption of the religious vocabulary identified with the rational vocabulary of the *Ethics* must also be emphasized: salvation is beatitude, i.e. freedom, conceived in the Spinozian manner as the maximum extension of the power of the spirit. Above all, love for God and God's love for mankind are now clearly identified. And this love, Spinoza goes on to say, is to be called, "rightly", "Glory", as in "the Holy Books". How is all this possible? How can we explain these truly mystical passages in the *Ethics*? If love of God and love towards God are identical, it's because of God's immanence. Spirit, insofar as it knows itself, is a part of divine understanding. These propositions XXXV and XXXVI often give rise to explanations reduced to paraphrases, and seem to greatly embarrass commentators. Significantly, Macherey breaks the linear order and studies XXXIII, XXXIV and XXXVII together, leaving XXXV and XXXVI apart.

A Mystical Reason? A Tentative Interpretation

The explanatory difficulties with this passage, and with the concept of God's intellectual love in general, stem from the fact that Spinoza is asking us to take a leap of faith and truly move into intuitive knowledge ourselves. In short, we can perhaps only understand these propositions by experiencing this "intellectual love of God" for ourselves.

Unable to explain, we would like to sketch out an interpretation here, or at least a few interpretative lines:

1) The intellectual love of God (whether it be love for God or God's love for Himself, i.e. for mankind) is both a love and an act of the intellect.

2) This experience can undoubtedly be summed up in one idea: when the mind achieves this intellectual love of God, it is because it experiences the identity between its being (defined by its singular essence, the essence of the mind of the wise man) and Being as such.

3) Finally, this experience is linked to the abandonment of all passions and feelings, and the reduction of all bodily affects to a minimum.

Let's take these three points one by one.

The identity of feeling and reason

As far as the first point is concerned, we're at the point where feeling and reason become completely confused. Up until Part IV, we used to oppose understanding and imagining, and therefore intellect and feeling. In Part V, this opposition disappears. Brought to its highest point, the intellect merges with pure joy, *laetitia* become *gaudium,* with the most perfect feeling, if we can still speak of joy, as Spinoza points out in E5P36S. It is therefore a radically new experience of the self, and indeed akin to mystical ecstasy. We might also ask whether this is not where we find an explanation of Spinoza's terminology: the second kind of knowledge is knowledge by reason, the third is "intuitive" science. Reason is an effort of the mind that works in the opposite direction to the real order of things. We go from *natura naturata* to *natura naturans,* from effects to causes, through all kinds of mediations. Imagination in this case is nothing other than the truncated, mutilated knowledge that most often obscures this difficult path. Every obstacle overcome is a joy, since it is an increase in the power of the mind. But joy presupposes the passage from less to more, and so it presupposes that there is more and less, inadequacy becoming adequacy, truncated knowledge to which we add the elements it lacks. In the third kind of knowledge, on the other hand, we follow the real order, and consequently even images are now grasped in their truth, since we think of them as necessary effects of the cause that is God. They no longer have the truncated, mutilated character of spontaneous knowledge. In other words, the separation between imagination and reason is no longer relevant. We are now in possession of a science that is not far from gnosis, if we sum it up as the identity of knowledge of the soul and knowledge of God.

Chapter V: Liberation and Bliss

Identity of soul and being

With regard to the second point, it is clear that propositions XXXV and XXXVI express this identity of soul and being. In each singular being and in itself, spirit meets God. Each singular being is thus a kind of monad that now expresses the whole of being (and here the points of contact with Leibniz could still be emphasized). As Michel Henry puts it: "There is nothing in the world where man does not find God. Where could the least sadness come from, if the infinity of things that exist is an infinity of witnesses that speak to us of God" (*Spinoza's Happiness, op. cit.*, pp. 102-103).

Michel Henry, who says in a pithy phrase that Spinoza is a "Platonic Jew", continues: "What is immanent, in us as in the world, is being, and our happiness consists in the feeling of being."

If the maximum power of the intellect consists in the adequate thought of God, of oneself and of things (to use the "Trinitarian" formula again found in the last scolie of E5), then the mind contains only the thoughts of itself, of God and of things, in due order; in other words, the mind is then identical to being itself in all its dimensions. This is why intellectual love for God is equivalent to God's love for man.

An (almost) metaphor for understanding

How is this possible? How can the part (which I am) identify with the whole? And above all, how can a finite mode identify with infinite substance? Quite simply—if things can be said to be simple—because the idea that I am (my mind) as an idea of the body, and neither the body that I have and am at the same time, is a substance. We must take Spinoza seriously when he says that there is only one substance (eternal and infinite). To understand this, let's first consider the attribute of extent. My body is an individual made up of a large number of individuals, themselves highly composed. What defines an individual? It's a set of bodies which, in terms of movement and rest, remain in constant relations, or variable relations only within certain limits. But what makes the individual are not these precise, material bodies existing at a precise moment, but these relationships, and this is why an individual does not change when the bodies that make it up are replaced by bodies of the same nature, etc. (cf. part II). But what makes the difference between the bodies that make up a swimmer's skin and the water in which he moves? Substantially speaking, nothing! There's a continuum. The difference is that the bodies making up the swimmer's skin remain inserted in the relationships that constitute the swimmer, whereas the water molecules have no constant relationship with the swimmer's body. If I want to define what my body is, then I have to be content with saying that my body is a certain number of relationships that organize the parts that characterize me. And that's all there is to it. These relationships are the essence of my body, that essence which is in God from all eternity. For obvious reasons, once you've understood the logic of Spinoza's thought, the same applies to my mind: its essence is a certain kind of relationship between the ideas that make it up.

Now, let's continue. Our swimmer from earlier can swim inadequately in the water. His movements are uncoordinated, they don't take into account the movement of the waves, so he makes little headway and drinks the cup. Because he knows little about the properties of water and has not trained his body in the practice of fluid dynamics, the swimmer is powerless, subject to his spontaneous ideas and panicking. He suffers under the action of external causes and feels like a foreign body in a foreign and hostile environment. Now consider a swimmer who knows how to swim. He composes the movements of his limbs in relation to the waves, he dips his head underwater and blows at the right moment, and raises it when necessary. He moves fast and is "like a fish in water". He has adequate knowledge and no longer feels like a foreign body. The rhythm of the wave helps him to move forward, and so the rhythm of the wave is an integral part of his movement. Between the wave and his limbs, between his limbs and his breath, between air and water, there is a relatively stable whole for as long as our swimmer swims. The part (the swimmer) and the whole (the swimmer in the sea) become one.

It seems to us that the intellectual love of God is just that! The moment when the individual mind no longer exists as a subject facing the object, the moment when the wise man's thoughts are so coordinated with the thoughts of the things that fall under his understanding with the idea of God, that the wise man's mind is as it were extended to the dimension of the whole world, and thus the part has extended itself to the whole (at least potentially).

We need to be a little more precise: the idea that constitutes the mind of the wise man is a finite mode. We also know that "the ideas of singular things or non-existent modes must be included in the infinite idea of God" (E2P8). The idea of God is infinite, but it's a mode. So when we say that there is a kind of infinite extension of the idea that is the mind of the wise man, we are not saying that the wise man becomes God (for he remains a man and does not perceive the infinity of God's attributes). The wise man only attains—and this is already enormous—the possibility of perceiving the idea of God at a glance.

Escaping from Passion

The wise man, by loving God intellectually, is a man capable of reducing his passions to almost nothing. This follows from the very definition of passions as inadequate ideas arising from the imaginary fixation of desire. Once we no longer have inadequate ideas, we are freed from the bondage of passion.

The following propositions complete what justifies the possibility of God's intellectual love:

E5P37. There is nothing in Nature that is contrary to this intellectual Love, in other words that can suppress it.

Indeed, intellectual love concerns the spirit when it is conceived by God's nature as eternal truth. We must not, therefore, apply to the spirit, considered in this respect, what applies to singular things that exist in a time and a place.

E5P38. The more things the mind understands through the second and third kinds of knowledge, the less it suffers from feelings that are bad, and the less it fears death.

In other words, the intellectual love of God does not come as an illumination. It is the crowning achievement of the mind's action to know, and it is this point that clearly separates Spinoza from the mystical tradition.

Mind and Body

The propositions we have just studied, says Spinoza (E5P40S), concern the mind "in so far as it is considered without relation to the existence of the body". Once again, it may seem odd to consider the mind unrelated to the body, if we remember that the mind is the idea of the body. So this whole passage is quite mysterious and perhaps simply not very coherent. But we can still make an effort to grasp what Spinoza is saying in a vocabulary with religious overtones: imagination does its work through perception, i.e. the body, but the third kind of knowledge is purely intellectual, no longer subject to the passions. The body is not denied, only that it no longer truncates reality.

Indeed, in proposition XXXIX, i.e. in the middle or near the middle of these propositions that study the mind "without relation to the body", Spinoza explains:

E5P39. He who has a body fit for the greatest number of actions has a Spirit, the greater part of which is eternal.

In other words, the power of the spirit is conditioned by the power of the body, or perhaps it would be better to say "expresses the power of the body". This would mean that the more powerful the body, the more eternal the spirit, and that I can only consider the spirit to be unrelated to the body in the intellectual love of God if I have a body and continue to take good care of it (*mens sana in corpore sano!*). And eternity is always present.

Or how about this: the more our body is capable of the greatest number of actions, the less we fear death! Why do we need to live and not rid our souls of the burden of the body? Simply because our spirit is all the more eternal, the more fully we live. A child is said to be unhappy when it dies, because its spirit has almost no eternity. And, therefore:

Chapter V: Liberation and Bliss

P39S. In this life, then, we strive above all to change the body of childhood, as far as its nature suffers and lends itself to it, into another that is fit for a very great many things and relates to a mind that is as conscious as possible of itself, and of God, and of things, and such that everything that relates to its memory or imagination is of scarcely any importance in the eyes of the understanding...

Conversely, the closer we get to supreme knowledge, the better we can live. Proposition XLII states things clearly:

E5P42. Beatitude is not the reward of virtue, but virtue itself; and we do not experience joy (gaudemus) because we repress our inclinations; on the contrary, it is because we experience joy that we can repress our inclinations.

Here again, the Latin text is perhaps clearer: *Beatitudo non est virtutis præmium sed ipsa virtus nec eadem gaudemus quia libidines coercemus sed contra quia eadem gaudemus, ideo libidines coercere possumus.*

This can be translated as: "Beatitude is not the reward of virtue, but virtue itself; and we do not enjoy it because we master our libidinous desires but on the contrary because we enjoy it, we can thereby master libidinous desires."

It is necessary, however, to pay attention to what follows. Spinoza does not propose ascetic conduct as an ideal (in the end, it would differ from ascetic, Christian or Stoic ethics only in terms of order (asceticism with a view to beatitude for the Stoics, or beatitude with a view to asceticism for Spinoza). The problem is rather to know which of these desires (*libidins*) must be controlled. The scolie of corollary II of proposition XLV of Part IV indicates that there is a reasoned use of pleasures that contributes to the health of the body and therefore to the power of the mind. The point is simply that these pleasures have an instrumental value and do not constitute man's ultimate end or beatitude.

We can more clearly identify the place of the intellectual love of God: it is an exceptional kind of intellectual experience, something that undoubtedly few can attain, but it is not opposed to the action that "ordinary men" can immediately take to live better. This is perfectly explained by Proposition XLI:

> *E5P41: Even if we did not know that our Spirit is eternal, it is nevertheless Morality and Religion, and, without any restriction, everything that, in the fourth part, we showed to relate to firmness and generosity, that we would regard as the first of things.*

It's hard not to think, once we've reached this point, that Spinoza's *Ethics* may not be all that far removed from Aristotle's *Nicomachean Ethics*, which distinguishes between moral happiness, based on the practice of virtue, and intellectual happiness, based on the contemplation of truth. We can't take this comparison too far, but it does highlight the profoundly classical nature of Spinoz's ethics and its intimate relationship with the conception of the Ancients.

Conclusion: Spinoza's Religion

To conclude, we should say a few words about Spinoza's religion. It doesn't make much sense to say that Spinoza is an atheist, even if it's clear that he sought to escape the accusation of atheism that would inevitably be levelled at him, and that he was able to disguise his real thought in a vocabulary more in keeping with a world largely dominated by religion or religions. Spinoza's motto *Caute*—rather like Descartes' *larvatus prodeo* ("I go forward masked")—is an invitation to go beyond the explicit text and understand propositions that could not be said in plain language.

Why is Spinoza's thought unbearable for the religious powers of the time (all religious powers, starting with the one that condemned him and excluded him from his community)? Spinoza doesn't say "God doesn't exist". On the contrary, he never ceases to affirm that "God exists". But Spinoza doesn't believe in God. He doesn't believe because God is not a matter of belief. It's because God exists that Spinoza doesn't believe in it, any more than it would make sense to say "I believe that 2+2 = 4", for the simple reason that 2+2 = 4, and that it's not a matter of belief. It's the evidence of God that reason can grasp and understand as a cause, of a God who is not hidden but present in everything, that theological authority cannot support.

At the same time, Spinoza lived and thought for a good part of his life in the company of dissident Christians, notably between 1660 and 1663, when he attended the *collegiate* meetings in Leiden, a sect recruited from among Anabaptists and Arminians, which held its college on the first Sunday of every month. Spinoza's philosophy can be quite widely accepted by a heretical Christian, say a pre-Pauline Judeo-Christian who doesn't believe that Christ is God. On the one hand, this interpretation could explain why not only the *Ethics*, but also most of Spinoza's works, are permeated by the opposition between false, superstitious religion and true religion, a religion of man, if we may say so ("man is a God for man"), summed up by justice and charity.

Finally, we're too accustomed to a Christian religion, instituted in particular by Augustine, which holds the power of human reason in low esteem (except when it comes to showing that the Church's enemies are superstitious, a specialty of the great heretic-buster Bishop of Hippo). But beyond the Gnostics, there's also a whole Christian tradition that makes reason the guide to true knowledge of God.

Clement of Alexandria (140-c. 220) defends a Platonic Christianity: knowledge of God is accessible only through philosophy (moral, physical), and Reason and Christ are identical. True philosophy is none other than the knowledge of Reason revealed by God to mankind in Sacred Scripture and in Christ. The true sage is the Christian, when he achieves the perfection of the moral life and the perfection of theological knowledge—in a word, to use a term dear to Clement, when he becomes a true "gnostic". The true gnostic is therefore an exegete, one who has the spiritual understanding of Sacred Scripture.

A fine apology for reason can also be found in Master Eckhart's sermon "On the Perfection of the Soul": "Whoever wishes to arrive at the highest perfection of his being and at the contemplation of God, of the supreme good, must have a knowledge of himself, as well as of what is above him, to the very bottom." And against traditional teaching, Master Eckhart places reason above the will.

Spinoza's thought should also be explored in relation to medieval Jewish philosophy (Gersonides) and the tradition of Latin Averroism. As condemned in 1277 by Bishop Étienne Tempier, this trend is characterized by the following points:

1°) The idea that God always acts according to an internal necessity of his essence, taken from Avicenna and in contradiction with the dogmas of Creation, Providence and human freedom.

2°) The eternity of species alone, to the detriment of perishable individuals.

3°) The union of the soul with the Intellect, the divine agent, and its return to him after death.

Among the Latin averroists, we should mention John of Jandun, who was a colleague of Marsilio of Padua, also a more or less disguised averroist, and whose ideas on the relationship between religion and the state are largely to be found in the *Theological-Political Treatise*.

So there is certainly a filiation in Spinoza's thought that deserves to be clarified. Just as the often astounding comparisons that can be made between Spinoza and Giordano Bruno, who is never quoted—he smells of burnt wood—but who might seem to have been paraphrased if Spinoza had had access to the works of the Nolain, which we know nothing about.

Do We Really Need to Conclude?

It's impossible to come to a conclusion when reading Spinoza. The first reading is an invitation to start afresh and discover new paths. A merciless critique of the illusions of free will, of the illusion that the self is the master in its own house, the *Ethics* is nonetheless an exercise in freedom, or more precisely, the path to liberation. To be free is not to obey our inclinations, since it is precisely these inclinations that are the result of the actions of external things upon us. To be free, on the contrary, is "to live according to the prescription of divine law" (E5P41S), not the divine law of an external, transcendent God, but "the law of nature", which is nothing other than the search for the good life based on a rational understanding of reality, of things and of oneself.

The *Ethics* seems to conclude with a hieratic figure of the wise man "whose soul is scarcely moved, but who, by a certain eternal necessity, is aware of himself, of God and of things, never ceases to be, but always possesses the true satisfaction of the soul" (E5P42S). But he is not a wise man indifferent to the world: on the contrary, he lives in the city and is attached to his fellow-citizens by the bonds of friendship, and if he is not moved, it's because emotion is the most unstable and fickle of the motives for action. Pity, though it may curb the cruelty of the cruel man, has nothing to do with true charity, a sentiment dictated by reason. Admittedly, the path that leads to this wisdom is "as difficult as it is rare", but "it can nonetheless be found". This wise ideal that "never ceases to be" is no more than an ideal, but it is an ideal that provides rules for living. Reading the *Ethics* is in itself a first imple-mentation of this rule of life, as it aims at knowledge of God, of things and of ourselves. If beatitude is not the reward of virtue, but virtue itself, then the same applies to the reading of the *Ethics*: it is in a sense performative, i.e. it achieves what it states.

ACKNOWLEDGEMENTS

This work owes so much to my companion, Marie-Pierre Frondziak, that I can't begin to tell you how much her rigorous reading of the manuscript, our lengthy discussions and her own research have contributed to thinking of Spinoza as a tool against alienation and submission.

TABLE OF CONTENTS

Chapter II: "The Nature of the Human Mind", or Mental Reality

Chapter III: Genesis and Classification of Feelings

Chapter IV: Man's Powerlessness: The Dynamics of Emotional Life

Chapter V: Liberation and Bliss

Best sellers Max Milo Editions

Hitler's banker, Jean-François Bouchard

Confessions of a forger, Éric Piedoie Le Tiec

The Koran and the flesh, Ludovic-Mohamed Zahed

Governing by fake news, Jacques Baud

Governing by chaos, Collectif

A political history of food, Paul Ariès

Mad in U.S.A.: The ravages of the "American model",
Michel Desmurget

Mondial soccer club geopolitics, Kévin Veyssière

Putin: Game master?, Jacques Braud

Treatise on the three impostors: Moses, Jesus, Muhammad,
The Spirit of Spinoza

TV Lobotomy, Michel Desmurget

www.ingramcontent.com/pod-product-compliance
Lightning Source LLC
LaVergne TN
LVHW051153060726
842526LV00014B/3183